the miseducation of a
90s baby

NON-FICTION

Cover by Matthew Revert

ISBN: 9781960988140

CLASH Books

Troy, NY

clashbooks.com

To my family, for letting me sell your likenesses for a few dollars. To my sons—we will discuss this later.

contents

the miseducation of a 90s baby

Khaholi Bailey

i am (not) my tits

BY FOURTH GRADE, some of my classmates were already "blooming," as Ma called it, as if our breasts were lying in wait in a cabbage patch. Some of the girls saw it this way, asking in the sanctity of the bathroom who had hair in places that they didn't last year. Other girls didn't bloom, they exploded. One of my classmates detonated right there in the locker room: she stood on the bench, pulled off her unnecessary sports bra and whipped it around above her head as her far-spaced starter titties waved for their first public appearance. What she bragged about as her early development was, to me, the last remnants of baby fat tucked under her chin and on her chest. I was unimpressed. And a little jealous.

But big breasts are something I was taught to not want. Should we walk past an older woman with breasts knocking together like dice, Mommy couldn't help but tell the same joke. Again. She would point her finger at one of her daughters and say, "That could be you one day! Because you know your grandma had those 'kajungas' (read: inconsiderately large breasts)." She only wanted us to have an idea of who we were before the kajunga gene from our paternal grandmother would define us– the grandmother who was apparently remembered for nothing else but her ill-fitting button-down shirts.

My older sister Lila's breasts started growing from the top. Fluffy tissue on the pectoral muscles. Small, yes, but all cleavage, gravity defying fat with no foundation.

"Together we'd have the perfect boobs," she said as we stood topless in front of the full-length mirror in her room. I shrunk at her freeness to be half naked in front of me.

"Yeah, we would." I stood closer to her, trying to picture what a conglomerate of our breasts would look like. We were referring to the fact that my breasts started growing at the bottom and stayed there. My skin was a thinning net under the weight of this fat, one side starting from my armpit and fastened to my sternum. My nipples were fluffy, rounding out what would otherwise have been a pointy tip. If you can imagine the snout of a poorly drawn greyhound, you could imagine my twelve-year-old breasts. Don't.

But, they grew. They grew pretty big. Big for my extra small build. Big enough for the boy who sat behind me in English to snap my bra every chance he got. "Stahhhpp!" I'd say if there were other kids watching. I'd bat my eyelashes and say "Ohmagod, you play too much," if they weren't. It became clear to me that breasts do not belong to women, but that women happen to be packaged along with the breasts. They stick out in front, opening doors and shutting them, attracting entitled voices. Older white women would stop me in the ladies' room. "What a figure!" They would look first at my breasts, then up to some vague point on my face, then over my bony shoulders and back to my chest. "What are you, a size zero?" I felt objectified, and it was everything I hoped it would be.

I learned to love the affections of older white women, as I had always been underweight, or as they preferred to call it, "trim". And once, by some generous calculation, a "brick shit house". Those who didn't happen to be an older woman called it "anorexic," among other uncreative terms. To make matters worse, it was from that same English class bra-snapper that I had first heard the term "fatty," which brought me to the sickening revelation that I was missing a big round ass, too. With no body to speak of, kajungas were the consolation prize I had to offer, assuming anyone who was attracted to me would be so in spite of my "holocaust skinny" frame. I've come to rely on my breasts and how many glances they received as a way to be heard without speaking.

I was more than willing to put my rack to work

in my day-to-day dealings. Out came the cleavage for any marginally special event. Why buy a new dress when I could push the girls together with the same old black bra with the molded cups and the front clasp? I wasn't particularly fond of this game, but was too honored to be deemed a player to reject it.

This sentiment was often the topic of conversation among my co-workers at that supermarket in Rosedale, Queens, where I ended up working in stints anytime I needed extra money. I was hired when I went there on an errand and the floor manager followed me around the store asking for my name (no, my real name. And it's cool if I had a man, he doesn't have to know). I gave him my real name after he offered me a job and put my real number on the application. Many of the young women who worked as cashiers had similar stories, showing up to buy groceries and being offered income. Between the midday and evening rush, we would find ourselves complaining about the male customers who tip too big and the ones standing across the street in front of the Crown Fried Chicken.

"I'd go out for lunch, but I can't go anywhere without those guys calling out to me," someone would say with her lips turned up at the corners. If she was really selling her frustration, she might even scoff and flip her hair.

"I know, right?" Another girl would throw her

hat into the ring. "And that tall one is always calling me Halle Berry."

This was not an exact conversation, but the exaggerated humble brags are difficult to remember. One could label such conversations as damningly ironic—the kind of inconvenient half-truths that span the multitudes of gray between the perceptions of men and women in potentially sexual situations. But the truth can be contradictory; as much as attention from boys and men had the ability to make us feel cheap and exposed, it was better than nothing. More than better than nothing, we waited for it, counted every single catcall and put it in a rotting hope chest in our minds. In my late teens and early twenties, the only feeling that rivaled the powerful discomfort of walking past a group of men and dodging catcalls was walking past several groups of men and being completely ignored. The attention didn't nourish us necessarily, but filled us up when there was nothing of substance around—sort of like grabbing a ninety-nine-cent pizza slice after the bar closes.

I would listen to this and slouch at the register, with my puffer coat underneath my apron and a shell of refrigerated air encasing me, film from dollar bills and soggy bags of chicken parts seeping into my chapped hands. Scanning items and that horrid, unfeeling sound that pervaded my dreams: *boop, boop, boop* marking the silent intervals or actively making the time go backward. I would half-heartedly flip through dusty celebrity rumor magazines, a vintage Playboy with a very pregnant Lisa Rinna or the weekly sale circular. Whatever was on sale, and whatever could be covered by the money in my tip jar was whatever my boyfriend Michael and I would be having for dinner. Us cashiers and grocery baggers would pass the time talking about ourselves, about other people's business, or by playing who'd you rather. "Ok, ok: would you rather raw-dog that light skin customer who never brushes his teeth, or be DP'd by the Mexicans in produce?" We commented on each other. "Those weren't as big before," they would say, pointing to my chest.

During my pregnancy my entire body was speaking to me, whether it was the cry of fatigue or the whisper of constant worry. Some could hear my uterus spewing rhetoric about how young women make life changing decisions based on their emotions. Others heard the whistle of my potential freefall into oblivion. My breasts were humming too, but soon they were barely audible. Eventually, no one could tell the difference as my growing belly eclipsed all other aspects of myself, perceived or actual.

The night after Michael Jr. was born, I woke up to waddle to the bathroom and look at my new self in the unforgiving hospital mirror. My stomach was wrinkled like a deflated balloon, my navel the puckered mouthpiece. My breasts were massive. They seemed to start from my neck and were bordered by my shoulders. Inside were serrated tiles of milk. My breasts were no longer for adoration or condemnation. For the first time, the value of my breasts was defined by what they were made to do. I had gone to sleep a girl, and through some haphazard variation of my mother's spell, I woke up a mammal.

My tits became teats with a working schedule. One would think that having larger breasts, even ones with their own responsibilities, would be a day at the fair. But carrying huge breasts was nothing like the pomp of holding firecrackers as I assumed; they were more like smuggling bundles of TNT. Just the thought of my son would trigger the milk to replenish. It would start tingling underneath my collarbone and spread through the chambers of my breasts. Should I have missed a feeding, they'd shoot out a round of the thin, sweet fluid, and I would often wake up in a sour smelling shirt with two dark bullseyes.

I'd wake up and change my shirt and place a nipple pad in each 32DD cup. I let them hide underneath my cashier's apron, a navy blue potato sack with holes for the neck and arms. I soon realized if I arrived earlier, I could call dibs on the newer apron, the black one that hangs from the neck and ties in the back, leaving my profile exposed. People smiled at me more. My tip jar was fuller.

Customers became mostly nameless acquaintances. Some would ask my opinion on products and throw thirty-five cents in the tip jar. Some insulted me: "I bet you could use a sponge like this to wash your bloodclot pussy." No contribution to tip jar. Some bragged about the groceries being for their ailing mother. Two dollars in the tip jar. Some only offered compliments: "Nice boobs!" Some bought us trinkets: "Will you remember me if I come back after I make a mixtape for you?" This one man said he was only paying with food stamps because he was rendered disabled after being hit by a car that jumped the curb. He smiled and flirted with a confidence I only sometimes had, worried I was too this or not enough of that for any object of my affection. He grabbed the shopping bag with his good hand and limped away.

For those customers who didn't tell us their life story, we gathered it from their posture, their outfits, the way they smelled. A young woman in her mid-twenties, a few years older than me, with a well-behaved child at her side approached my register. She wore a sundress with an elasticized waist, a modest garment that showcased her smooth legs and simple sandals. "She's the type of woman who has all her bills paid on time," my co-worker said. She didn't contribute to my tip jar, a small, recycled plastic container with some of my own money in it to inspire customers to add more. I didn't want her to. I wanted people like her to be oblivious to my goose-bumped skin and my attitude of the tired and poor. I noticed who added change to my tip jar and knew why: the man with the crazy eyes who bought my smile with five-dollar bills, the man who asked for my email address to further discuss 'The Word,' only to renege after considering his marriage, the elderly man who insisted on walking me home, only to show up at my door to walk me to work the next morning. He appeared from thin air on a bicycle, his long legs stretched out over the pedals as he cruised over the bumps in the concrete: "Wheeeeeeeee!" See? He wasn't that old.

I was over it. Especially when I learned that other cashiers, girls who had not been working as long as I had, got raises. A whole twenty-five cents more per hour. I brought this to the attention of Andrew who had been co-managing the super-market with his brother for years. His brother was more introverted and non-confrontational, but the last time a girl went upstairs with him she stomped out of the store yelling "pervert!" never to be seen again. I hardly had any memorable interactions with Andrew or his brother, except for his brief commentary on my name: "Khaholi, huh? What an ugly name for a pretty girl."

He unlocked the door that opened to a narrow staircase, so steep it was almost a ladder. The only people who frequented upstairs were the head cashiers who made the schedule and the Dominican vendors who smoked cigars while their invoices were reviewed. On top of the stairs was an attic of an office with a low ceiling, boxes upon boxes of paper, and narrow sliding windows tinted black, which offered an eagle eye view of the registers and the exit. He took a seat in a distressed pleather office chair and offered me the milk crate parallel to him.

He pulled my file and made easy conversation:

"So, you're in school, right?"

"Yeah. Hunter."

"What's your major?" He asked as he fingered through sheets of paper.

"English."

From there, he segued into what he was doing when he was my age.

"When I was like nineteen, twenty... I used to date this woman. An older woman,"

Ew.

"Plus, she would give me gifts, sometimes stacks of money. So, it was a win/win."

I was starting to speculate how they chose to name the Head Cashier.

Feeling gross for only having nodded along to his pitch, I flew down the staircase and back to the stark lighting and cold air of the register, a whole twenty bucks per week richer, only to see the limping guy with a CD jewel case in hand. I couldn't decide whether I was more annoyed with him or sad for him: Do I just say thank you? Should I start telling people to fuck off? Before I could decide who to be, he was at my register and leaned in to speak.

"Uh, Miss, is Jocelyn working today?"

I paused for a moment, confused, before I pointed toward my coworker at a distant register.

He hobbled over and handed her the mixtape, made especially for her.

Jocelyn and I would sometimes walk to the bus stop together at the end of our shift. But first, we would dump our tip jars and slide the coins to count our worth for the day, then match them up with the weekly sale items: whole gaming chicken, eighty-nine cents per pound, block of frozen broccoli, one twenty-five, three-cup bag of rice, one eighty-nine. We would sweep through the aisles and collect our groceries, ring each other up and pretend like a few barcodes weren't swiping, to type in a price of twenty-five cents. We would grab our bags and walk out of the store, eyes away from the sausage party forming in front of the Crown Fried Chicken.

At least one of the men in the group would notice us and wave. This time it was a man I had long ignored to the point of playful haughtiness. He waved and I prepared to give an exaggerated eye roll before he called out, "Hi, Jocelyn!"

Jocelyn looked enough like me, but better. She was Barbie, all cheekbones and doe eyes, and I was the flat-footed knockoff on the shelf below. I would be considered exotic looking from time to time, though it never seemed like the right time.

I felt the static of two young men behind us, walking quickly to catch up. One appeared on either side of us, and I wondered if we were a joint acquisition or if I was being wing-manned.

I started quickly, trying to shoo away the

annoyance with, "We both have boyfriends." A line that never really worked, but only acted as a wall which some men didn't have the energy to scale.

"I don't," Jocelyn pounced. The man next to me became quiet, and the other closed the deal by getting her phone number.

We continued walking to the bus stop to take us to Far Rockaway, where we both lived. She told me about the men in her life, including her baby daddy and the only male cashier she was closing in on. Eventually, she shared a lamentation on her insecurities: *how the fuck does everyone else have tits and ass now?*

In two years, I was pregnant again. At the supermarket I tried to hide my growing belly under large sweatshirts and by leaning forward on my register (I could still pass as a still a stick figure from behind). I was ashamed to be pregnant for the second time at twenty-two. I already hated forcing a smile as customers made small talk about their children and said something equivalent to, "but you don't have to worry about that yet." I felt more mare than human, allowing my pussy and tits to behave as a vagina and breasts. A second child would make me more than a baby momma, but a whole entire mother with a family. What a waste.

When the secret got out, I sobbed. Then I thought I'd use it to my advantage. I would poke out my stomach when people would arrive with two full carts of food, trying to communicate that my register would essentially function as a self-service line. Instead, I'd watch the groceries pile up beside the plastic bags. Wordlessly, I was told that it was my decision to get pregnant, just as it was my decision to work a physical job. So, I squatted and lifted and bagged, without tips, because there was nothing the tippers could hope to get in exchange.

I gave birth again, except this time without the epidural or the 'less potent' epidural alternative that could only be described as a hallucinogen. I writhed along with the metal sphere of fire forcing its way through my body, and looked up at Michael and the three nurses who seemed to be studying me. Was I pushing the wrong way again?

One of the nurses looked at the others and said, "She looks exotic."

"She," meaning me? The person two feet from your face getting her perineum split? Finally, someone noticed.

"Well, yeah you should see her mom," said Nurse No.2.

"She must've had her very young," hating-ass Nurse No.3 added.

"No," Michael said, "she's well into her fifties."

"Stop! No!" the nurses said in disbelief.

I asked God why he didn't just kill me and get on with it as my portal widened to present a second baby boy. He was quiet and content and went quickly to sleep, like he was sure he was now where he needed to be.

I again had more milk than my son needed. However, my first pregnancy left me with enough stretched skin on my chest to fill the milk ducts to capacity without changing my cup size. When I stopped breastfeeding, the fat in my chest dried up along with the milk. I held on to the C-cup bras for as long as I could. I readjusted the straps until the large cups lay flat and empty on my chest. I told myself that my breasts weren't deflated, it was just the particular brand's awful sizing. And all the other brands in the world made bras that were clearly misshapen.

My breasts were shriveled triangles, starting from the unfortunate fold of skin pulling from my sternum. I had no tits and no ass, and I stood with my pelvis jutting out and to the side, a posture deformed from carrying babies on my hip. My body did what it was made to do; it was shapely enough to attract a man who fertilized two eggs, which I paid for with two breasts. I was spent, a twenty-three-year old Old Maid.

It was my mother who told me to let go of my old bras.

"If you wear a bra that doesn't fit, it doesn't help them look better," Ma explained. "I know it's hard. I didn't let any man see my breasts for the longest time, but trust me, they will come back."

She pulled down her shirt and I was shocked to see her youthful breasts. They were easily a C-cup, something I never noticed before. I felt a jolt of hope for my genetics. And a little bit jealous. Who was she to have great boobs that would just sit on the shelf?

"How long did it take for them to bounce back?" I asked.

"Hmmm, I don't know... maybe when I was forty or so."

"Forty?!" I felt the embers of hope disintegrate. Ma gave a half-smile and a shrug, one that explained I would be forty faster than I thought.

That conversation with Ma left me with conflicting feelings of hope and acceptance. I started throwing away my big bras, all the while mourning my breasts and blaming karma for their demise. I wished I could take back laughing at the portrait Lila drew of our friend's flat body, with a rectangle for a torso and two lowercase U's at the center. I lamented over every cleavage-centric article of clothing that I never cared to wear but now could not. I even waited for breasts to come up in conversation so that I could retell the epic tragedy of my own. I backed it up with old photos on Facebook that I pretended not to have bookmarked beforehand. I'd show people an old picture of me at a party wearing a spandex dress and that old black push-up bra with the molded cups and front clasp. I'd widen my eyes to warn other women: this could be you one day.

My worth was debatable, but some nights as my shift ended at the supermarket my worth was in the shopping bag I carried home. I would get off the bus, last stop, and walk to my apartment as the frigid air from the supermarket and bus slowly flaked away. I would plop the groceries on the counter and wash my hands, soap stinging the cracks in my palms. I'd pick up my son and bring him to my nipples, made large and rectangular. My eyes traced thin red rivers in my skin as each tug nicked away at the rocky reserve of milk. My chest flattened, my self relieved.

I would then unload my discounted groceries and start dinner. I'd clean the chicken in the kitchen sink, its bones and bulges not unlike a baby's. Nine hours' worth of smiling and jeering, of defense and defeat worth almost nothing in cash but a break from oatmeal or pasta. Nine hours of proof that I still had it, even if 'it' was only worth discounted poultry. My family served, I'd say a silent grace: Thank God for my dry, calloused hands, my aching feet and my spent, flattened, priceless tits.

mcdeity

MY SISTERS and I would pray out loud with our heads down and our hands clasped, reminding each other of the things we forgot to ask for:

"Oh yeah, and please make Grandma come back to life. Amen."

"Wait!"

"Oh yeah, and a troll doll. Rainbow hair. Amen."

Satisfaction was a matter of being polite and waiting for our turn to be heard, for corpses to resurrect.

I also knew that when I heard "Assalam Alaikum," I should reply, "Alaikum Salaam." I didn't know what those words meant, or what language I was speaking, but it was like having a secret password, should a man in a bow tie greet us on the street. Daddy joined the Nation of Islam as an adult and eventually taught us how to

pronounce "Assalam Alaikum" and not much else.
Ma was in the Nation of Islam for a short time
during her childhood. All she remembers was a
sermon about the mothership returning to Earth
(she doesn't remember when it is scheduled to
return, but she does remember that whitey is not
invited). There may not have been enough religion
between the two of them to go through the rigama-
role of learning Arabic, to sort out their possibly
different takes on polygamy, or to discuss the even-
tual fraying of the Nation of Islam into two separate houses. But they could agree that their
daughters looked adorable in the plaid skirt and
thick white stockings that was the uniform of the
local Baptist day school.

Inside that preschool classroom came the
commandments: Be quiet, Stop moving, You must
not want lunch today, huh? For any infraction our
teacher, Ms. Betty, would cancel mealtime and grab
potato chips with her fingernails, reserving steady
eye contact for one student per chip. She possessed
a vigilance matched only by some cunning character from the Bible, I'm sure. Even when met with
a seemingly impossible mystery, Ms. Betty was on
the case:

"Who peed all over the bathroom floor?"

A hot-faced silence all around.

"No one? It just got there by itself?"

With no one willing to jump on the grenade,
we all lined up in front of Ms. Betty's kneeling
assistant. When I made it to the front of the line, I

didn't look at him. Maybe that was when I first noticed the picture of a man with long brown hair and a gaze of dissociative empathy. It was not the same man in the picture above my parents' bed— that man wore a shallow hat embroidered with glittering crescent moons and stars, and I thought he looked like a fine maker of good dreams. Maybe I was thinking about these two figures, or that I was hungry, or wondering who peed on the bathroom floor as I held the teacher's assistant's shoulder for balance. I pulled my white stockings back up over my hips.

My sister Lila and I compared notes about her afternoon in the adjacent classroom. She told me that it was her classmate who had the wet-tipped penis and therefore urinated on the floor. Case closed. It was the same little boy who was always in trouble with Ms. Betty and her assistant, even though he never seemed to do anything wrong. I was relieved, yet somehow astonished at Ms. Betty's lack of tenacity. I hadn't even considered that she would give up upon hearing "no." She was a fraud, and a flake. If her heart wasn't in anything that she preached, perhaps I had to readjust my budding faith toward something tangible.

According to the Trolls commercial, I could rub its potbelly and expect magic to fly out. No more memorizing prayers, no more dead men's gazes imploring you to be better than human when no one else had to.

My prayers were answered. Ma bought me the

doll that would compact temperance into a Happy Meal. I rubbed its belly and wished for a rainbow, just like the girl in the commercial. Nothing. I asked again, this time massaging the doll deeper as if trying to dislodge a blockage in its bowels. Nothing. I demanded it, fighting the realization that I was duped by a lump of shit.

———

By the time we moved from Brooklyn to Long Island, Grandma was still dead and we no longer prayed together. With no rosary to count or verses to read, I spent my nights staring at the cartoon wall decor stickers parallel to my bed. Through the slightest force of intention, physics would bend and crack, allowing the dalmatians to romp about the wall in watery frames of motion. I knew I saw this in my imagination, though since my eyes were wide open each time, it was more than fantasy. The ease of creation was as natural and reliable as any of my senses—some provable, adaptive trait of human vision.

But who cares about meditation after you're introduced to cable TV? Cartoons aired every day, not just Saturdays. Plus, Daddy bought us a Sega Genesis, on top of the Nintendo we'd inherited from our teenage sister, Walida. We watched all of this on the new giant television that seemed to be at least five feet high and six feet wide. It eclipsed the entire bay window in the living room.

"What a terrible spot for a TV," Ma said during one of her visits (she and Walida stayed in Brooklyn along with most of the furniture). "It blocks this whole beautiful view."

The TV compensated for blotting out the sun by offering other interpretations on faith and death. I was given my first notable impression of Hell by watching *All Dogs Go to Heaven*, a children's movie seemingly inspired by redemption-themed parables and the work of Martin Scorsese. The main character, a German Shepherd named Charlie, keeps an orphan girl he manipulated into living with him in squalor and committing petty crimes. Also in the pimp game is the Dog Mob, headed by a merciless bulldog in a tailored vest. In order to procure the lucrative orphan, the bulldog invites Charlie to a party orchestrated around his murder. Drunken Charlie sings and sways and is not suspicious of the blindfold placed on his eyes, even as a car revs and its headlights diminish his shadow. Charlie notices nothing until he is in Heaven because, as the title suggests, even human-trafficking dogs go to Heaven.

But all children do not, Uncle Muff explained. "You're old enough to go to Hell at twelve years old," he said as he stood in the kitchen and ran off the rules for salvation, none of which I remember. I do remember one of us serving covert sass, asking why twelve and not eleven or thirteen? "God had to draw the line somewhere," he shrugged.

Uncle Muff's warnings were all but reiterated

by Mrs. Lee, our babysitter and tenant. Her three kids would sit on the carpet with their legs folded and a hardcover children's Bible on their laps. Mrs. Lee sat in front of them in the same position and spoke as plainly as the plastic band that kept her brown hair out of her face:

"Those people would pray like this," she said, with her hands palms up and shoulder width apart, "so God would not listen."

I didn't realize at the time that "those people" were Muslims. I also didn't realize that the portrait that hung above my parents' bed back in Brooklyn was of the Honorable Elijah Muhammad, leader of the Nation of Islam. The picture was hung up high underneath the crown molding, further adorned by the two smaller pictures that hung beside it. It was a realistic painting, though likely stroked with the propagandized beauty of a leader unburdened by his responsibilities, or the guilt of his illegitimate children.

Although Mrs. Lee didn't answer any of my personal questions about God, her kids taught me a lot: I learned that all secular music was wayward except for "I Saw the Sign" by Ace of Base. I learned that playing the game Limbo mocked God and the realms of the afterlife, and that I was a lesbian because they once saw me kiss Ma on the lips. Most of these lessons were spontaneous, inspired by my wanton instincts, like singing along with the radio on the way to the Kingdom Hall.

Whenever Daddy was late coming home to

Long Island from work, we had to go to the Kingdom Hall for weeknight worship, and the dread built up in my chest as the afternoon turned to evening. Worse, I had to wear thick white stockings, at least that one time anyway. I pulled them up and they stretched slowly like cold taffy, finally landing mid-thigh. I showed Mrs. Lee, hoping I could get away with wearing jeans or not going at all.

"No one can see that with your skirt down," she said. "Let's go."

On another night we rode to Kingdom Hall as Mrs. Lee's nephew, a boy slightly younger than me but old enough to profess his crush on me, sat on my lap in their crowded sedan. The awkwardness of our sitting arrangement began to dissipate once I succumbed to the harmonies of Boys II Men's "I'll Make Love to You" as it played on the radio. This turned into a singalong in the backseat (her kids seemed to know the song pretty damn well). Mrs. Lee waited until the song was over to turn down the volume and start her sermon.

"Do you think that's an appropriate song for you to sing?"

If I had sung that song in front of my own mom, she would have let me belt it out with the growling, church soloist passion that was nineties R&B. If Ma would say anything at all, it would have been about the differences between love making and sex that would have embarrassed me enough to never sing the song again. One thing Ma did tell me was that religion is about control, that it allows people in power to predict what their constituents will do and think. In an unintended sense, I thought Ma was right: I vowed to never sing or even relax around the Witnesses. I attended the Kingdom Hall meeting with folded arms and a blank stare that went totally unnoticed.

Such incidents didn't stop the Lees from giving me my very own children's Bible when they moved out. I opened the stiff new golden hardcover to find kind words and pictures of people of all races basking in a lush garden with domesticated lions at their feet. I felt acknowledged. I stroked its pages and inhaled its dryness, put it down, and never opened it again. There was something comforting about having a big book of answers and being saved, but being a Jehovah's Witness was hardcore. The logic seemed to be that the consequences of interpretation or disobedience are too great, as God in his infinite creativity doesn't limit the punishment of man to a lake of fire. I learned that God could take every memory and bud of imagination in a fury that will seem like a flash of light that changes the Earth's prism to a single shade of gray. God can give you disease, kill your family to test your faith, or to my painful confusion, banish a soul to nothingness for eternity.

But if you become nothing, and can't remember your existence, did you ever exist?

Why are we the chosen species and not the apes?

What makes us different from mosquitos?

Or viruses?

And what about the people who died millennia ago still awaiting Judgement Day? Are they counting sheep into the trillions, rubbing their elbows raw against their coffins, trying to reconcile their cliff-hanger endings? Is that respite from going straight to Hell, or is it like waiting on a roller coaster that tick-tick-ticks toward the peak of the track as you count your regrets once the parking lot comes into view?

Ma tried to preemptively answer my existential questions by saying that God was an idea. She relayed an anecdote about when my sister said she didn't want to join her classmates in teasing another kid. That was Him: God.

Another family member never directly explained his beliefs, but I did overhear him talking to his friends one night as they watched a basketball game: "All the shit I've seen, there is no God." He contradicted his statement many times before and after.

No matter how inexplicable the unseen world was, religion was always there, poking at us like a pebble that found its way inside our shoes. It was in the smug faces of our classmates who got to leave school early for Confirmation, in the diverted eye contact of the adults who asked us where we went to church. I was primed to belong, to have the answers, minor bouts of starvation and molestation be damned.

Instead of visiting a new church on a typical Sunday, we went for its grand holiday production. Inside the white coliseum of a church, we found friendly people buzzing in anticipation for the show. Behind an inconspicuous door was a theater of Broadway proportions and modernity. We found seating central to the stage as the lights dimmed low and the stage lights turned up. The first vignette started with three young women chatting in an apartment, and it went something like this:

INT. Kitchen, Every Town, USA. Night.

Three young women stand in the kitchen of a luxury apartment. They are chatting and settling in for a night of conversation and snacking when there's a rumble outside the front door.

Girl #1
    Did you hear that?
    Girl #2
    Hear what?
    BOOM! Thieves break in. The lights fade out. The women shriek before we hear the sounds of their deaths: POP! POP! POP! The stage lights crescendo.
    EXT. Outside of Heaven's gate.

The three young women stand, slightly bewildered. They understand that they are dead, but maintain high spirits.

Girl # 3

Welp. Let's see if Saint Peter is letting people in or if we gotta wait 'til a few people leave.

Girl #1

Wait... I don't know if I'm on the guest list. I got pretty p'd off when my folks divorced, and I said some bad things about the Lord.

Girl #2 and Girl #3 nod, figuring that divorce is tougher to reconcile with than being shot to death. To absolve Girl #1's doubt, they break out in Whitney Houston and Mariah Carey's "When You Believe."

The song fades out, and there is a moment of fearful anticipation. Then "Hallelujah!" begins to play and the three women jump and embrace and make their way through the gleaming gates.

The audience is jubilant, and a single Denzel Washington tear rolls down Daddy's cheek.

In the next skit, a would-be adulterer enters a hotel bar and lays out his plan to the bartender. He is so psyched about cheating on his wife that he is blind to the bartender's red skin and horned skull. The bartender lends an ear and some encouraging words to the man before giving him the key to room number 666. The audience laughs, and Daddy tells us it's time to leave.

Was he made uncomfortable by the implication that a less than pious husband will meet hellfire?

Did he think that a God truncated into a wafer-thin lesson was bound to dissolve on our tongues?

Other people have tried to convert me by explaining the importance of religion in bite-sized portions. Years after that church production, my high school boyfriend came back from juvie and had been rehabilitated for real this time. He had endured his sentence by jerking off with socks filled with shampoo and going to the youth ministry. He called me to testify both to the natural feel of a slight lather and the redemptive powers of Jesus Christ. He explained that any girlfriend of his must be a Christian. I assumed he would discard his faith after the last meeting with his probation officer, though I hoped he wouldn't. Religion for him was an anchor lodged in papier-mâché, but an anchor nonetheless.

After our conversation, I lay down to sleep staring at the elderly tree outside my bedroom window. Wispy fears of damnation swarmed my mind, not just because of my born-again boyfriend, but from the portrait with the painted blue eyes on the wall of my preschool and from my classmates who told me that being without a religion means, "God is not with you." I prayed for a sign. Per usual, my prayers were answered.

I went to sleep and opened my eyes to my bedroom, which was dim with blue light. A dense wind pushed from every direction, forcing my uncertain gait. I knew intrinsically that I was dying, that I was wavering on the median between infinity and fire. I held my hands out, hoping to grab a hold of something familiar. I found nothing but doubt and regret.

I woke up in my bed to find the same wretched tree outside my bedroom window, in the same brick house in the same cul-de-sac. Maybe I went back to sleep to dream a similar dream, one that was clear in its moral, but just as quickly ignored. I could hope to dream a different dream, where I knew exactly where to place my feet to keep from falling, where everyone prayed the same way, where we knew exactly who was watching us from behind the stars and the moon. Instead, I lay in the familiar shades of darkness and let it wash over me.

baby's first relaxer

AS PUBERTY APPROACHED US ALL, it became clear that my classmate Roxy, with her medium brown skin and long mermaid waves, was destined to rack up those in-class deliveries of carnations every Valentine's Day. Daffodil, the new girl with the slack jaw and stiff plaits, was destined to pretend she has a super hot boyfriend who happens to live in another town. I feared I would land somewhere in the middle.

Roxy leaned over our lunch table to demonstrate their differences. Her smile was wide and bright, save for gaps of missing teeth that mirrored the sliver of space between being an unbridled kid and an asshole. She wound her hand back and slapped Daffodil's braid. It was the kind of chunky braid that started with a ball barrette and ended with a clip barrette.

"They look like cojones!"

The other Puerto Rican girls laughed first, and the Black girls laughed after—maybe it meant 'shit' or 'balls'? Either way, I was next in line for a relaxer, and it couldn't come a moment sooner.

My older sister Lila was first to get one. She walked in the front door one morning with a bobbed haircut, curled and styled like a middle-aged woman who slept in plastic rollers. I hovered my hands around her hair knowing instinctively not to touch it. "How does it feel?" I asked. She said the weight of her hair was gone.

Before the perm, Lila would wear cornrows like me. Ma would unravel my braids, lay me on the kitchen counter and wash my hair in the sink. Then section, then detangle, then re-braid my hair to look like the inner workings of a kaleidoscope. The everyday geometric shapes on my scalp were more fitting for a celebration, like the return of a sun god or the merging of two kingdoms. The white girls in my class saw it the same way, tracing their eyes along the primordial design. They'd marvel that my mom could do this every morning, as their moms only brushed their hair back into a ponytail. My hair could not be done in the morning like theirs could. Firstly, my hair had as many disparate forms as water. Secondly, my parents split by the time I entered kindergarten, leaving Ma every other weekend to wash, section, detangle and braid the hair of three little girls. Something had to give.

Enter Lisa, Daddy's new girlfriend. She had dull eyes and long nails the same color as the filter on her Newports. Lisa couldn't braid hair. Learning how to would seem to her archaic, as her perforated hairline revealed that she got a relaxer every four weeks. Lisa was the one who suggested that my sisters and I get a second piercing in our ears. Lisa also suggested that we refer to her as 'Lisa Mom' and that we get our hair relaxed.

The thought of getting a relaxer made me I think of my mother, the one who gave me an African name and replaced her own relaxed hair with locks. "Don't call them 'dreads,'" Ma explained. "That's a term 'they' use. This hair is not dreadful." But, the thought of getting a relaxer also made me fantasize about blowing bangs out of my face, a la Stephanie Tanner. I was sold. I was eight years old and ready for the inevitable: the chemical castration of my ethnic identity.

When it was my turn to visit the hair salon in Queens, it was an early morning. I was glad to be the first customer, as getting my hair relaxed was embarrassing in conflicting ways. I didn't want the world to see my feral, unbraided hair, just as I was ashamed for thinking that my natural hair was shameful. I don't remember looking in the mirror as the beautician parted my hair into bushes and slathered on the warm white creme. She protected her own skin by wearing plastic gloves.

When the relaxer was rinsed out, I could feel

water running down my scalp for the very first
time. The water tickled and I felt a bit open, probably from the small abrasions dotted along my hairline. The weight of my hair had been literally lifted;
I felt bald save for the fringe of hair tickling my
cheeks and my shoulders. My hair didn't seem like a
part of me. I couldn't stop petting it or picturing
myself on a children's relaxer kit with starched
pigtails and impossibly rosy cheeks. I walked into
that salon a little girl but left with a switch in my
hips, a bad little bitch.

Every six weeks was the same routine. Since I
had been initiated, I felt comfortable going during
peak hours. On Saturdays the salon was packed:
older ladies getting roller sets, teenagers getting
finger waves, men selling jewelry out of suitcases,
Hot 97 on the radio. The younger beauticians
would turn up the music when their favorite songs
would play and keep the volume high as they spoke
cryptically about men. I was too young to hear the
details about what happened in a parked car while
R. Kelly played on the radio, yet old enough to alert
the beautician when the tingling on my scalp
progressed to piercing heat. If the stylist was more
committed to 'laid edges' than avoiding chemical
burns, she wouldn't rinse out the relaxer as the
manufacturer directed. Instead, she'd spray oil
sheen onto the spots that were burning to dilute
the relaxer and the pain. It was a gamble that could
result in barren hair follicles, or the kind of silken

hair that made interested boys ask you what race you're mixed with.

The white and Hispanic girls who were awestruck by my cornrows were now replaced with other Black girls lining up to comb my Good Hair. My classmate and fellow relaxee, Tiffany, forced a brush through my hair, tugging out a handball-sized tuft. She wore an expression of guilty horror which met my practiced, nonchalant face.

"Does this usually happen?!" Tiffany looked to the brush as if it were a bloodied knife.

It doesn't happen to you? I thought.

"Yeah," I grabbed the hairball and walked casually to the trash.

In no time, all that bang-blowing and hair flipping left behind a trail of thin and crunchy strands on my shoulders, my pillow and around the bathroom sink. Eventually, parting my hair to the side revealed a scalp-bearing wedge like that of a sixty year old man.

We realized relaxers were not necessarily low maintenance. It required moisture and hair wrapping, brushing the hair out and then around the curvature of your head while smoothing it and securing it with pins: a feat of psychomotor coordination that I never cared to master. I was still young and clinging to the freedom of only caring about my looks peripherally, so my hair slowly changed from that of a relaxer kit model to that of an exhausted mother. The chemicals could not stop the strands from growing upward like leaves arching toward sunlight.

My mother kept quiet about our straightened, thinning hair I until I asked her. I don't remember what she said, but I do remember how her eyes narrowed and that she spoke through clenched teeth. My mother's sentiments were more cathartic to my subconscious than I realized until that point. I didn't want to allow another woman's opinion to supersede my mother's. I didn't want to spend hours in a beautician's chair just to look like a more acceptable version of myself. I wanted to reclaim my hair as a celebratory identifier, one that would frame my face in a crinkly, coily halo. By eighth grade, I had grown back my natural hair.

As it turned out, no one saw my hair as a halo, and neither did I. I was too old for braids that converged into beaded pigtails, too lazy and tentatively proud for a temporary straight style. In the year 2000, with no YouTube tutorials to guide me, I ventured out on my own with arms stretched out before me. I bought the pricey two-for-a-dollar butterfly clips at the kiosk in the mall and let them nest in my bush. I stumbled into French braids that looked like fraying rope, ailing cornrows in the front with a poorly picked out 'fro in the back, and the infamous double French rolls that urged two of my friends to come out and say, "You have the worst hair!"

With nothing to lose, I tried temporary straight styles. I spent hours with my high school best friend, Martine, in Ma's basement with a hot comb on the gas stove. Martine's own natural hair could be straightened neat and thin using a plug-in curling iron, whereas I had enough hair for two adults and a baby. She successfully straightened some of my hair while other sections fell, scorched and blonde into the sink.

"You look like a 40 year old lady on the bus," she laughed, and she was right. My fresh hair style already looked a few days old, and a decade too late. It looked tired. I was tired.

I relapsed. In tenth grade I got a relaxer and had my hair cut like Toni or Halle. I consoled myself by thinking a relaxer wasn't a complete disregard for my ideologies. A short cut would make me an individual, which if I was honest with myself, was the crux of why I committed to having natural hair when no one else my age did. My afro was in part an affectation, something to indulge my ego. A straightened pixie cut would be a loftier rebellion.

Having short hair was freeing. I would wash it, slather on moisturizer and walk out the door. I finally fit in, yet still teetered on the fringes, which I'd call my comfort zone. I was hoping my newfound lightheartedness would fortify me as I got my six-week fix, and technically it did. I was able to go to the salon with dignity, but the entire time I would torture myself by trying not to think about a scene from the movie *Malcolm X*.

Malcolm X was born Malcolm Little and was known as Detroit Red, but moving to Harlem only made him a big fish in a bigger pond. Aiming to look like he belonged, he visited a barber shop for a "conk". Moments into the hair treatment, Malcolm begins rocking in the salon chair, breathing through his teeth like a woman in labor. On his scalp was pure lye: used for liquefying animal carcasses, making plastic, and in the 1950's, permanently straightening hair. It probably felt like minuscule whips separating his brown skin from itself, leaving scabs that will become something altogether new. When the lye is rinsed out, Malcolm smiles with all of his teeth, smooths his hair with his palm and says, "Looks white, don't it?!"

I would replay that scene in my mind as I sat wrapped in a beautician's cape. It draped over me like a plastic circus tent, my head springing from its center like the main attraction. I read and reread old issues of Hype Hair to avoid the ghost of Malcolm Little in the mirror and to quiet the voice of Malcolm X in my mind.

I decided the solution to my dilemma was not to stop relaxing, but to do it at home instead. I would buy the ironically named African Pride brand and lay out the kit: the plastic gloves, the activator, and the cream. I'd put on the gloves, wrap a towel around my shoulders and apply petroleum jelly around my hairline to protect from burns. I'd part my hair and slap on the creamy crack.

During a trip to K-Mart to reup, I went straight

to the ethnic hair aisle and picked up some more shame-in-a-box. The woman at the register smiled wide when she saw my purchase.

"This used to be my brand!" she said. "You know, back when I used relaxers."

I looked up to her hair; it was matted in the custom of overworked and underpaid discount store employees. But it was hers. I took it as a sign and went home to relax my hair for the final time.

I announced to my boyfriend at the time that I was going natural and watched as his eyebrows gathered in the middle of his forehead. "It's cool," he said tentatively, "as long as you're not one of those girls who thinks having natural hair means not combing it."

His statement carved a nick of doubt in my mind. I already understood that revealing your most natural form to the man you're dating is more nerve racking than disrobing for the first time. To reveal to him that not only do I have coarse hair, but that I committed to wearing it in public could be seen in the same regard as gaining too much weight or a damning family secret. It wasn't my decision to wear my own hair that I began to doubt, but my appeal to him, to men in general, to all people who see natural hair as a domineering political statement. In truth, however a Black woman decides to wear her hair is inherently political. The only decision allotted to a Black woman is whether she wants her hair to agree with what her lips say. I was tired of the double-talk.

I toughed it out through another regrowth process, never once considering doing the 'big chop'—cutting off all of the relaxed hair and essentially starting off bald. Luckily, this time other women stopped perming their hair in droves (whether I hit the trend or started it, I cannot say). Strangers encouraged me in the beginning stages by sharing their hair care routines. It usually involved gentle cleansing, three deep conditioners, eight moisturizers, reciting a love poem to their scalps and maybe the Black Bill of Rights.

If all else fails, there's always hair gel. What I had once thought was exclusively for Puerto Ricans defines my curls to an admittedly more socially esteemed texture. I wish I could be repulsed when men look at my smoothed edges and ask for an itemized breakdown of my gene pool, but I'm not there yet and may never be. But I never cared to treat my hair like a religious idol or become a spokesperson for the revolution. I just needed to look like myself.

I am more relaxed with my hair than I have ever been. I remember waking up next to my boyfriend on a Sunday morning, not worried about which direction my hair was leaning. We were establishing a real closeness, the kind that made me ditch my uncomfortable shoes and contemplate wearing my mouth guard to bed. My hair was one of the last aspects of my appearance I let go of, but I did. Unceremoniously, nearly unconsciously. That quiet Sunday morning, I focused on the love gaining strength inside of me, which manifested the love lying beside me. I didn't know how I looked, but I felt beautiful. My man turned to me and looked at my uncovered, festive, feral, spongy, coily, covetable, incredible, dreadful, original, gel-free crown and smiled before whispering, "Wait a minute... do you have nappy hair?"

the puppy episode

BOYS WERE IN THE PERIPHERY, attached to the back of my head by a slack leash. Every so often, some testosterone-driven oddity would pull me taut and make me wonder, *Now why on Earth would he do that*? One of those times was in kindergarten, when I watched a boy set up a makeshift display table and place a worm on top. Armed with a plastic spoon, he sliced the worm into bits. Each piece of the worm twisted away as I wondered if it became its own worm or if we were witnessing desperate final spurts of kinetic energy. This was the ticket price to being around a boy: a novel, often gross, adventure. I turned away in disgust, but not before somewhat admiring him. Mincing the worms made him rebellious, aggressive, and showy, everything I was not. My fascination with boys was like being scared of the vastness of the ocean but knowing from your intuition that it is wise to settle near the shore. I knew that even the shallowest bodies can pull you under the current and keep you from breathing.

Girls were agreeable, like Joyce. When Uncle D and his wife divorced, Joyce came to play housewife while D got used to being a single parent. One of the very few perks of being a single father is the ever-growing line of women, with children and without, who miss the satisfaction of having a man ask for seconds. Joyce played the part to a T: she did laundry, took splinters out of our hands, and took us on outings to pass the time. She even did so in miniskirts and sheer hosiery. She was wearing one of these getups one day as I watched her and D sitting at the kitchen table. She was reading something to him with the attentiveness of a mother or preschool teacher. The only words that were spoken were on the page, but under the table, D was rubbing his palm over her thigh.

Soon after in school, I sat next to my third grade classmate, Sandra. According to her my breath was rancid and her friends couldn't pick me to be on their team in gym class without her objecting. Still, my general indifference toward her left a gap for the occasional slip of friendliness when no one was watching. She was explaining some of our classwork to me with a doting patience I didn't know she possessed. I also didn't know why she was explaining it to me, only that she wanted to. I wanted to show gratitude, so I looked down at her nylons, skin colored, the kind that Ma said was too grown for me to wear. I was hesitant to touch her, but I was above giving her the satisfaction of hearing me say "thank you." I placed my hand on her thigh and slid it up and down as static formed and popped underneath. My hand was left tingling with that feeling of potential energy unrealized. She didn't respond, so I rested my hand where it was.

I hadn't realized the sexual game Uncle D and Joyce (and me and Sandra, apparently) were playing. I hardly even knew what sex was. Ma said sex involved a "special touch," leaving me to think that men had some secret-society handshake that gave life. I saw the preliminaries of this magic trick once when I walked in on Uncle D and one of his girlfriends from the adjoining bathroom door. Someone's big brown ass was fixed midair, the same way time and motion seemed to stop when I jumped off the swings. So, sex was rolling around and apparently jumping and landing on your partner. I had learned about penetration after, from a scribble on a desk of a crude phallus and a 'V' above the caption "open wide!"

There was another game they were playing. The one where Joyce pretends that schoolwork is checked and dinner is hot effortlessly. This game of voluntary and gratifying service didn't always start and begin with mutual understanding. Last I remember of Joyce is sitting with my cousins in the backseat of Uncle D's minivan as she rested with her feet on the dashboard. D told her to move her feet, but she debated. She felt she earned the right to put her feet up, I assume, so that's where they stayed. Without another word, D rolled down the passenger side window, and in one swift move, flipped her ballet flat off her foot and onto the highway. There was maybe a moment of silent shock before my cousins and I were smacked by laughter. We laughed at the gesture, we laughed at its boldness, we laughed at her frozen face. Joyce made a bit of protest and then retired to look out to the stretch of road she'd surely be hitting soon. And that was how I'd remember her: a shoeless foot, and a vibrating rage clogging her throat.

Every time I turned around, there was another link in Uncle D's chain of fools. We met one standout desperado when a car pulled up parallel to the edge of his lawn. An unexpected sighting such as that in the suburbs was a reason to peer out the window and see if we recognized the car. We didn't. A slim woman in a miniskirt emerged from the driver's side and approached the house.

She introduced herself with a bright voice and smile. She gave her name, which sounded vaguely familiar. D had mentioned her and her crazy attention-seeking antics, but not why he kept her around. This was her, in the sinewy flesh. She said she came to meet us and to take us to the mall for portraits to give as a gift for Uncle D. My cousins, sisters and I were home alone, bunkered under preteen ennui, when we had to decide whether or not to get in the car with this stranger. Pro: a trip to the mall may inspire her to buy us things. Con: she might send Uncle D one of our fingers in the mail. We decided to go, perhaps the tie breaker being that Lila had a chance to wear her new baby blue kitten heeled sandals.

On the way to the mall, Desperado made small talk and asked what shows we watched. We shrugged and answered *Friends* at which she playfully scoffed. *Frasier* was her show of choice. It was sophisticated humor she went on, as I studied her short, curly brown wig and ultra-toned limbs. She had the kind of body that made me wonder if she used the gym to let out her aggression: if so, she was angry often. It also made me feel for her, as she didn't even have the sense to know that she wasn't really Uncle D's type. Aside from his ex-wife, most of his women were *thick* thick, the more stretch marks the better. Desperado was cheery, financially stable and articulate. She would be a dream for many men, just not the one she was trying to impress. I could see how she identified with the title character of *Frasier*, with his Italian shoes and ten-dollar words to describe his two cents that no one seems to want.

We arrived at South Shore Mall and headed to the portrait studio. We agreed to a theme of simplicity with a white wall as a backdrop. We posed and contorted and smiled and picked the least pimply picture of the bunch to have printed and framed. Desperado returned us home and drove into the sunset, never to be seen again. Still, she left an imprint on my mind about the woman I

would never want to become. We told Uncle D
when he came home, to which he smiled tentatively, as though he had the urge to count all of our
fingers.

Longing for men seemed to me a precarious
matter. Still, I had crushes on boys for as long as I
can remember. My first crush was a neighborhood
boy named Terrance, an older boy who would play
with us kids outside of our building in East New
York, Brooklyn. I would twist my leg as though
putting out a cigarette with my tiptoes, bat my eyes
and say, "Hiiiiii Terrance." In kindergarten it was
Ian, with the easy smile and the blond buzz cut. I
confessed my love to him while singing "Wild
Thing," a required morning sing-along, for some
reason. I pointed to him when it was my turn to
sing: "I think I love YOU!" He faux fainted out of
his chair, and that was all I needed. I didn't even
circle 'yes' when my crush, Ram, all onyx skin,
pearly whites and perpetual placement on the
honor roll, passed me a note in second, third and
fourth grade. I ghosted him elementary style,
ignoring his note and zooming out of the classroom after the final bell. Rejecting him was the
strongest wielding of power available to the gender
that customarily waits to be chosen. But I liked
him. I liked him a lot. I liked him so much that I
spent the night of the last day of elementary school
singing Janet Jackson's "I Get So Lonely" in my
bed in regret. I missed my chance and now I'd be
alone forever. If I was honest with myself, I would

have noted that although I liked him, I didn't like him nearly as much as I liked Power Rangers.

The problem was that boys could leave your heart open and bleeding, and only come around to collect those drops of blood when they need it. I didn't see my fate as a woman with one shoe on her foot, or creatively chasing a person who very much wants to be inside of me but would never let inside their home. An ancient avenue out of the conundrum of being attracted to males was better identified to me by Ellen DeGeneres.

By 1997, Ellen was no longer the blonde on TV that my uncle sometimes stopped channel surfing to watch until the next punchline. She was many things, including a comedian, a writer, and a producer, but apparently, she was mostly gay. I have seen and known women like her, with their Johnathan Taylor Thomas haircuts. I may not have had the vocabulary to describe a woman like her, but I didn't feel I needed to—terms like cousin, teacher, neighbor sufficed. When Ellen said "Yes, I'm gay," and I couldn't turn on the TV for weeks without seeing a reaction, I stopped to think about what it was. The thought of lesbianism was, to me, just a vague jumble of two female bodies underneath a blanket making clicking sounds as their acrylic nails gleefully knocked against each other. At nine years old, I hadn't questioned my sexuality before, but I didn't like boys the way my friends and classmates did, which was openly, underneath the swing set on top of puddles of saliva. Ellen's plight was to me like a commercial for medication for an ailment I had not previously considered, but the list of symptoms made me stop and think, *perhaps I should talk to my doctor about Lesbianiz.*

This misguided definition of my sexuality stuck with me forever in kid time, which is to say a few weeks. I felt the weight of the secret. It became so heavy that it permeated to Lila, with whom I share extrasensory perception. She would randomly ask Ma how she would feel if one of us came out, to which I would telepathically scream at her to either shut up or to blurt it out and put me out of my misery. What I really needed was a clear list of parameters to understand my feelings. In the 90s, homosexuality was identifiable by the way a man or boy behaved. A man with too-perfect posture: gay. Two teenage boys sitting next to each other on the city bus, without the empty middle seat for their overflowing testosterone: a couple very much in love. What made girls and women gay was not as clear. Androgynous girls could be considered a tomboy for their entire childhoods, a phase they were trusted to grow out of shortly after menarche. That alone made it clear that women and girls never have to adhere to any sexual title longer than the associated feelings last. But soon, just like my love for Power Rangers, I thought of it less and less until I didn't think about it all. My sexuality quietly and naturally calibrated as time passed.

While I was sure that I didn't like girls, I still forced a crush on a boy in sixth grade to keep up.

This boy was confidently, sporadically disrespectful to our deserving teacher, but since he and I were in the top tier reading group, I could foster the idea that there was a misunderstood, tortured genius under his crumpled face. He would never pursue me, or even talk to me, making him a good candidate for a crush. He was also ethnically ambiguous, the kind of boy I was supposed to crush on. Someone I could write about in the diary Ma bought me, because what else did girls write in their diaries?

Then it was the other boy, the tall dark and handsome seventh grader with the *S* curl and diamond earrings. I saw him making out with a girl on the way out of school one day, so I was sure to act sullen and disappointed the whole ride home. I opted to sit alone on the school bus, looking out the window. Yep, that should do it.

Besides having to ramp up my sexuality, middle school also ushered in a school day without recess. We all pretended to like that concept because it meant that we were getting older, but I suspect that we missed playing. Girls still played as they got older, but the games were so subtle, many of us seemed to forget we were playing at all or who we were in the first place. Joyce was playing the part of a woman who was with a man who wanted her, when it was possible that he just needed anyone at the time. Desperado pretended to be a giddy woman eager to surprise her man, but we knew her actions were more worthy of a restraining order than praise. But, as long as you perform, no one cares.

This notion seemed compounded after I discovered porn: the acting was bad. I couldn't fathom how many of these acts were anything like the once jarring scribble on the desk. But who cares? Once dial-up internet connection replaced pixelated pictures and stalled videos, came the notion of how a girl's sexuality should be. Those images stayed with me, and seemingly everyone around me well into adulthood. "All women like women. It's natural," men like to remind me. They usually suggest this with a glint in their eye, like they can hear that funky bassline that accompanies all brewing threesomes. Years later, a man even asked me about it on our first date, because alluding to penis-in-vagina sex would have been crass.

"Are you bisexual?" He said, with a light laugh to make it sound like it isn't a big deal, but just enough to give his excitement away.

"Are you?" I blinked and waited.

"You're not supposed to ask me that," he laughed and pushed his chin back just enough to seem surprised, but not enough to convince me that the answer was no. What he did tell me was that he successfully jerked off to gay porn once, but only to prove to his gay brother that homosexuality is a choice. Okay, then.

In his defense, the performers he watched weren't meant to be men or women, per se. The point is for the performers to be a template for viewers to mentally photoshop their fantasies. It is tempting to tease out the insidiousness of this display of our most connected form, but we misplace our expectations and create disconnection regardless of the medium. In my late twenties, for example, a woman that I met at a writing group invited me to a poetry slam. We quickly ordered drinks and began building friendships the way girls do, by telling each other quasi secrets to rush intimacy. I was having a hard time keeping up with the who's who of her romantic woes until she shook her head in frustration. "No, no. My ex is a girl. We're all lesbians. Well, I don't like to define my sexuality, but I mostly date women." I wondered if my perception betrayed me. It was like when I read a few works from a particular writer and didn't find out until the third or so essay that he was married to a man. I skimmed the other essays for clues I had missed and took a glance at his author photo, as though I would find him wearing shiny shorts and an ironic mustache.

Still, no group is more identifiably coiffed, arguably, than cis girls and women. While our animal counterparts are the drab colored, often duller looking half of the species, human females know how to attract more dancing hopefuls and the better choice of nest, a strategy materialized in stereotypical gifts for girls. A standout favorite of

mine was the Tinkerbell beauty set. It came with
peel-off nail polish, perfume and plastic pumps.
Every item was impossibly bright pink which made
it special, though it was common enough to be sold
behind the counter at the bodega along with the
condoms and tampons. I appreciated the notion
that pink and polish and pumps could harness the
idea of a woman, though this was not necessarily
the same woman I pretended to be when I changed
the diaper of Lila's Baby Alive doll. It was evident
that women who acknowledge, embellish and own
their sexuality are not playing by the rules, but the
rules were changing, even for pets: my tamagotchi
was guaranteed to marry and lay eggs by simply
surviving to the end of the week. The other pet I
owned was a literal rock, so the pressure was off for
him, too.

The nuances of sexual selection and magnetism
are also lost on the simple worm. I confirmed later
that the worms the boy split with the spoon were
not budding, as they reproduce sexually. These
intersex creatures lay in excreted goo, of course, and
spray sperm on each other's eggs. How equitable.
No mating dance or display of strength, just the
perpetuity of the species. This simplicity is in itself
worthy of the boy's disdain, or at least made them
disposable in his display of fearlessness, as he had a
role to play, too.

Some of us garnered such attention seemingly
effortlessly. That same woman I met from the
writer's group was the kind of person near

strangers hovered around like jets that needed to be refueled. She generated warmth, especially when their eyes were fixed on someone else. After the poetry slam, we started for her downtown apartment with an expanding group of her friends. It was located in the portion of Manhattan that still featured cobbled streets, where warehouses are divided into smaller spaces made for stuffing suburban migrants inside. The apartment opened to the kitchen and was deeper than it was wide, leading to the large living room and then the backyard. We sat on the couch and watched *The Bachelor* reunion special before we got into more robust introductions of her roommates, all of which came from Central Casting: Gangly Brunette who worked in marketing, Square Jawed Man who worked in marketing, and Femme Dude in Tight Shirt, also in marketing. While Femme in Tight Shirt rolled a white paper for his roommates and a few of us guests, the woman from the writing group asked me in nineties sitcom fashion if it would be ok if she slipped out of her work clothes into something "more comfortable." She came back in what would have to pass as her lounge clothes: a gauzy see-through pink top, cut off denim shorts and Calvin Klein panties peeking out from the waist. Queue the audience track: "Whooooo!"

We went to the sliver of a backyard and stood beneath string lights and a haze of late summer heat, marijuana and cocktails. She stood in the center, all of us looking at and addressing her. When most of her roommates and guests announced their early meeting and went back inside, the one-woman show went on with a small and captive audience. With some encouragement, she stood downstage center beneath the white string lights and recited an original poem.

She spoke in a practiced cadence. She touched her throat and chest and closed her eyes as though she only existed as the speaker of her poem. When she opened her eyes and fixed them on me, she was back in her body. I attempted to break away by looking into my empty cup, but there it was again. Unfaltering, penetrating eye contact. My heart was heavy, armpits percolating. I was a child. She was an initiator, one who could look at another grown woman and squish her with her thumb.

I excused myself to the bright, large bathroom to try and quell the wild expression in my eyes and sober up. I decided to announce my exit before I further revealed myself to be a person who went to a commuter college and had a low tolerance for intoxicants, including awkward, oddly appreciated sexual advances.

When I returned to the backyard, she was rubbing her hands up and down another girl's thighs. This was not a discreet move made under a table or desk. She knelt down between her knees and bit her lip in between sentences.

"I'm gonna head out," I announced, while

sizing up the woman in front of her who was enjoying the massage and idly sipping her drink.

I wondered how much of her demeanor stemmed from confidence and how much was an aspiration. Of course, it didn't matter as long as she didn't break character. She was who I pretended to be when I wore the plastic heels and bed sheet gown. I imagine she was the provocateur the boy with the spoon wanted to be too. She seemed to see herself as someone worthy of admiration, as the integration of every part of herself and surroundings, the parts that would dissect a worm and the charmed and revolted parts that would watch and wonder.

digital
degeneration

ON CLOUDLESS NIGHTS, I would stare up at the night sky with Uncle Muff as he would point out planets and prominent stars. He would arrange the mystery of the sky into men and women and shapeshifting creatures. The longer I gazed, a faint dotted line would appear to connect the constellations, acting as cords through which we could perceive the larger picture, some confirmation from the ancient readers of the skies who deemed this the Era of Information.

Until the year 2100, Earth is in the constellation of Pisces, the two fish that Venus and her son Eros transformed into to hide from an enemy, according to the Greeks. With this and other constellations, one can find their cardinal direction on Earth as readily as their position in the cosmos. These suns and planets were, to me, once invisible but since unmissable, though that never stopped me from gazing with my valuably untrained eyes for a constellation of my own discovery and meaning. Deciphering messages in the night sky was similar to staring at the neon colors on the back of my eyelids as I laid in bed at night. I would perceive and connect things that I assumed were only present in my mind, but were in fact all around. These constellations, connections and myths born out of the human condition may change form, but seldom change. This, to me, was the meaning of infinity.

That is until one day in 1998, when Daddy brought home a box. Inside that box was the internet: infinity plus infinity. A black hole of possibility, lassoed by the phone cord in our kitchen.

Daddy bought the internet home in order to help my sisters Lila, Mani and I with our homework, of course. It had nothing to do with the fact that the Johnson's got it first and my sisters and I flocked to their computer as if email was some Promethean gift. My sisters and I wanted the internet to be better connected to the future, of course. It had nothing to do with the fact that we didn't have a subscription to the Spice Channel, or that the cable company would scramble the images, forcing us to discover porn through a Picasso-style collage of nipples and latex. Whatever our motivations, we knew that the internet would be a game changer, something that would replace all other things: game consoles, libraries, investigation of the darkness above and within.

Our Hewlett Packard desktop evolved from processor to starship. We turned the computer on, endured the electronic gurgling and arrived in Internetland bright-eyed and vibrating. But after opening the Welcome to America Online! email, we discovered that the internet was a rather barren place for the recreational user. We traveled in and out of this new realm, supplementing our entertainment in more primitive ways. We still played Street Fighter on Sega, and when I did, I didn't just choose to play as Chun Li: I was her. I mimicked Chinese gibberish when I won and felt Pavlovian blows to my gut when I lost. This of course was built upon the tradition of playing Barbies complete with backstories and motives, of watching movies and calling out, "I'm her!" when the princess arrives, her prince somehow my prince. Playing through characters served as a prerequisite into the digital dimension, where you can transform completely, instantly, autonomously. We soon discovered that all that was needed to play pretend on the internet was a screen name and a subscription to AIM, or America Online Instant Messenger.

On AIM, my little sister and I based our screen names on an episode of *The Fresh Prince of Bel-Air*. Carlton, or HersheyKiss, developed a heated digital romance with the faceless BrownSuga (who was unbeknownst to him, his sister, Hilary). My older sister, Lila, followed suit and named herself MsMocha. There was no option for pictures, making every user either more deceptive or more honest. These profiles served as the pre-Google way to spy on your loved ones. It was through AIM that I discovered that one of our relatives is "bisexual and loving it!"

With my new identity and not much else to do, I wandered into a chat room. Chat room names were compiled on a list, and each room was given a name to function as a dog whistle for certain demographics. There were rooms called 'Around the Way' and 'The Barbershop.' I never heard the term 'honky tonk' before then, but after being called a nigger in that room, realized it had a similar in connotation as 'The Saloon.' The rooms were organized like a group text, with a robotic administrator announcing all those who arrived and departed. There were often two or three conversations going on simultaneously, and it was up to the user to insert themselves into one. Often, I wouldn't have to. Someone would inevitably type "a/s/l everyone" and I would respond with my age, sex and location. I would usually say New York, but other times I found excitement in being someone else from somewhere else. As for age, I figured I was not in a place for children, so I would make myself older, more mature, like twelve or thirteen. The combination of my screen name and age would garner attention and before I knew it, someone would send me a private instant message.

It was a game to see how many instant messages would pop up on the screen, how many people were interested in a preteen named Brown. I would read their messages and decide who was better to spend the evening with. Would it be the 25/m/Texas? Or the one who pretended to forge a bond by typing something like, "U seem so mature. Can I get to know you?"

No matter who I chose, it was the same conversation. It would start off gingerly, like "What brings you to 'The Bodega'?" and end with something that would make me look over my shoulder and ensure I was alone. "U got a pic?" These words were not exciting, yet they were enlightening. I was the equivalent to an immigrant seeking out conversation in order to better understand the language and customs of her new home. I learned that in Internetland, people weren't 'people' per se. People live in your neighborhood, go to the same supermarket, chat with you about the weather. Those from the internet are a sort of Frankenstein composed of our collective base desires. And pedophiles. Lots of pedophiles.

There were public service announcements warning us about these predators. In these commercials, there would be a plucky teen sitting on a bench waiting for her cyber boyfriend, all while her thoughts play in the audio track in the background. *I hope he's as cute as his picture. I think I'll finally tell him I love him too.* The color washes from her cheeks when she realizes the fifteen year-old she thought she was connecting with is actually a middle-aged man sporting a horseshoe balding pattern. The only other stories of meeting someone online involved DIY basement dungeons and laws named after the doomed children. Nonetheless, I considered not sharing my true name, location, or pictures as fine measures of safety. As expansive as the internet was, it was not a man in a trench coat walking along the perimeter of the playground. It was just a set of wires hanging underneath our desktops.

Armed with geographical distance and a growing fluency in this new language, I kept frequenting chat rooms and began to experiment with my responses. After growing accustomed to men asking a/s/l, I would answer with all lies, then go the unnecessary mile of sharing my imaginary Jessica Rabbit measurements. I would go to AskJeeves.com for help translating terms I didn't understand, like why so many of these guys offered to "break my back." My online personae made it so that infinite varieties of myself could live and evolve on the internet. It was my introduction to the Matrix paradigm, dirty-talking simulations all the way down.

Search engines could have also told me that it was the Babylonians who deemed our era Pisces before the Greeks, named for a story about a precious egg in the sea that was rolled to shore by two fish. When it hatched, it revealed not a newborn animal, but a fully grown goddess. The Mesopotamians had their own take on the constellation, though we can at least agree it looked like fish to our comparatively starving ancestors. Pisces, one of the largest constellations and one of Earth's main astrological influencers, also happens to be one of the dimmest. It's nearly unobservable to the amateur astronomer, if that matters at all, as the act of reading the stars is an accidental lie. Our modern astrology is based on the geocentric model of the solar system, and therefore defunct; unless you side with the argument that astrology is for humans, and our literal viewpoint agrees with geocentrism. Now there's countless search engines with countless answers to back you up either way. We don't know shit, all the way down.

This is the era in which Jesus was said to atone, marking a return of the idea of the internal Heaven. It was a call for humanity to go inside ourselves, and inside ourselves we did go; we discovered our passions, our curiosities, compounded our knowledge, and emerged two thousand years later swollen with possibility. We birthed a kind of god of our own—half-human, half-asshole with a penchant for intoxication of all kinds, and swaddled it in cellophane. Google is a better predictor of my obstacles and destiny than the position of the stars. iPhone, therefore, I am.

My personhood was a labyrinth of which I was unsure of the starting point, of who played predator and who was the prey. My sister must have felt this too, sculpting her alter ego by shooting wildly in every direction. The difference between us is that I did it while looking over my shoulder,

keeping implicit secrets. My sister typed with aban-
don, laughing through her hyperbole. "I'M A
PORN STAR!!!" she once typed. The pulse of the
statement pushed her back into her seat as she
laughed and looked at me, her unwitting accom-
plice. To my surprise, the person on the other end
seemed to believe her. I figured that there must an
idiotic streak in all men when there's any mention
of sex. It hadn't occurred to me that the people we
conversed with could be other children.

Maybe watching Mani lead this 'man' along
helped me decide that it was safe to go further than
typing flirtatious words of which I hardly knew the
meaning. The connections were through wires,
nothing that could jump out and grab me. Almost.

One night, I was online chatting with some
person who asked to share a photo of himself. I
looked over my shoulder to find only the small light
above the stove and the kind of darkness outside
that makes everything feel open, wild. I said yes.

Internet visuals were mostly pictures, and the
image would inch its way down from the top of the
page, moving more slowly the more you wanted to
see it. The picture began with a few horizontal lines
of dark brown. A few seconds in, I could make out
wood paneled walls and dim lighting. It was not the
kind of lighting one would associate with romance;
it was the type of darkness that insinuated that
whatever happened in that room would be a secret.
At that moment, the internet wasn't boundless. It
was more like two people communicating through

tin cans connected by a string. There were no more fractal versions of BrownSuga—just me, in my pj's.

More of the picture downloaded. I saw a mop of brown hair. Then closed eyes. Then a Cheshire grin. More picture, more hair, this time an oasis in the middle of his flat chest. He was an adult. I was afraid—of getting in trouble, of being embarrassed, of seeing something I couldn't unsee, of not being able to put the lid back on the box. In the hodge-podge porn I was accustomed to, men were trape-zoidal smears presented in a photo negative, their pupils and eyelashes a stark white against the void that was their eyes. But on the screen was the image of an actual, unpixelated man. A man who wanted a girl, a girl who thought she wanted to be seen as a woman. I was transfixed, both guilty and innocent, repulsed and excited, rewarded and punished.

What I saw next, I wasn't sure. In the fore-ground was an impossibly long, fleshy object. I had yet to see an actual penis, and I imagined them as pointy rods with Hannibal Lecter-type skin flaps along the shaft. What was on the screen was some pink phallic thing that had the rubbery, raw quality of an uncooked hotdog. I shut off the internet.

The stars, and everything else made of carbon, are encased in lore and wrapped around perhaps a singular perfect sphere of truth. Pisces, this net of information, passed down for millennia through trillions of lips to hard-of-hearing ears and distorted perceptions. The internet wasn't the infi-nite space I thought it was. Or maybe it was, but no one wanted to delve into the mysteries of the universe: everyone wanted to be in a virtual dive bar. To find ourselves through the night sky or within, we will find one contradictory projection of Us. Old lessons repackaged in ones and zeroes.

momma needs marijuana

I FELT TALL. I was Alice in Wonderland after she ate the mushroom, my head swaying with the treetops. I tried to keep my hollow body from tipping over from the gust of wind coming from somewhere inside my living room.

"Sorry, she's not really a smoker," my friend and supplier Rick said, looking away from me so that his cousins might do the same.

The blunt we smoked was a departure from my own joints, which I would clunk together in a triangular shape using notebook paper. I would snuff out my own concerns about smoking the paper's ink, inhale a poorly packed nub of weed into my throat, hack it up with alarming intensity, and repeat. Rick's cousin, however, parted a cigar along its seam, replaced the tobacco with weed, and rolled a blunt in a geometrically perfect cylinder. The smoke ran unobstructed to my lungs, and apparently to my frontal lobe, making everything —the sounds of their voices and the traffic outside, the weight of the air, the origination of my thoughts—somehow separated by a thin film, or by some unconscious will of separateness. It was a feeling both odd and familiar, the memory of a dream; the fountain of youth and the wisdom of old, a vibration that was never created and will never cease. I inhaled a language of images, the same tightly coiled communication which informs surrealist art. It is more than a language; it is a state in which the barrier between what is outside of you and inside, is lax enough to inhale the thoughts of others and exhale the rotted ones stuck between your teeth.

You feel me?

Stifled laughter and darting eye contact all around.

When describing this feeling, I refrain from using the phrase "felt like," for it attempts to secure a sliver of tenability. I have no desire to appear reasonable, for many things we deem reasonable make less sense than drug-induced experiences. We trade our time for money to buy food that grows freely on trees; in *Sex and the City 2*, Carrie and the gang traveled to Abu Dhabi where they sang 'I Am Woman' in its entirety. Evidently the answers to life's burning questions are not outside of ourselves, because out there is an enigma wrapped in a menacingly positioned enema. It seems that the answers to life's burning questions are to be posed to one's self, 'one' being both singular and encompassing the collective consciousness of all of humanity.

How about now?

"Drink some milk," Rick's cousin suggested as I wiped my face with the hem of my tank top. I wanted to care, to at least check for boogers smeared on my cheek, but etiquette was somewhere far and away, sixty feet or so down at my ankles.

"Look how she holds it in," Rick said, honestly endeared.

They passed two more blunts, I stepped out of reality. I wanted to philosophize on the nature of being, or to see if Rick and his cousins were aware that time had suspended, but all I could hope for was that the thought bubbles forming above my head were legible. But back to my point before I lose my train of thought; to find the answers to life's burning questions, just ask Uncle Muff.

Anything could spark one of Uncle Muff's meandering lectures on life and morality. One minute my sisters and I would be making jokes or eating a meal when Uncle Muff would lean against the faux-wood countertop, cross one foot in front of the other, and touch his index finger to his thumb, meaning it was already too late. We learned not to ask questions and not to resist, for it only made it harder to see the swatch of sunlight on the wall dim into the evening, harder to keep our thighs from falling asleep on the wooden dining chairs. Whether the catalyst was one of us alluding to something mildly "unladylike," or something said on television, Uncle Muff usually covered one of a few topics:

• Don't talk to strangers, especially ones with lost puppies.

•Don't treat your toys carelessly. When he was a boy he had none.

•Don't dress like tramps. It attracts creeps.

•Don't play beyond the crack in the driveway. It separates our property from the wilderness of the street.

•Don't walk away when he's monologuing. It's disrespectful.

During one of his sermons, my sister Lila asked how he knew what the hypothetical predators he was warning us about were thinking. Uncle Muff answered that he spent many a night conversing with rapists, kidnappers and drug dealers during his stints in jail. So went the moral of that particular lecture; he had it on good authority that the Bally Total Fitness commercials are dangerously seductive.

Along with watching commercials with unnecessary close-ups, marijuana was also baited as a dangerous pastime. It led not only to blackened lips and red eyes, but to a dimension too bleak and abstract for us to maneuver. One of us asked him plainly if marijuana is a gateway drug as the public service announcements in question claimed.

"Yes. I've seen it happen." He may have leaned over the stove to check on his famous slow cooking french fries—the Other Cancer Sticks. They were transparent, smelled of stillness and would burst into a crumbly oil-bomb in our mouths.

"You smoke," Uncle Muff continued, "then you just want to go higher and higher."

Maybe then he would duck his head into the refrigerator and peel a few American slices out of their package to make sandwiches. For an appetizer, he would pinch open the plastic wrap and replace it with a turkey cold cut, and eat it in two bites without his lips ever touching.

"Before you know it, you're doing angel dust, and your brain is stuck on crazy forever."

Then Uncle Muff may have wiped his fingers on the towel that forever rested on his shoulder before clenching a cleaned margarine container filled to the brim with whole milk. He'd bring it carefully to his lips, pinky finger out, perhaps to demonstrate his previous proposition on the value of etiquette.

Eventually my sisters and I started piecing together subtle clues. We knew what to look for because of the After School Specials he taped on VHS and made us watch again and again. Uncle Muff's Riker's Island recipes was one of them. His scent was another. It lingered on his stubble and on all of his belongings. It was a warm but flat scent, pungent and specific but not exactly stinky, and ran parallel to the smell of Irish Spring.

His friends always arriving relaxed and happy, despite taking the nearly two-hour drive to visit, should have been another clue. Lonnie, my favorite of the clique, with his Chuck Taylors and lank locks, smelled like Concentrated Muff and knew exactly how to relate to us grade school kids when it came time for small talk: "You know how when you go number two, you can't help but go number one?"

Uncle Muff's other best friend Rich poured the wholesome on too thick, also raising our concerns. We could enter the room and catch a glimpse of him mid-conversation before he noticed our presence. His forearms rested on his knees, and he seemed to speak quietly and seriously about the kind of grown-up business I didn't bother eavesdropping on. The moment Rich saw our faces, however, he turned into a big, purple dinosaur.

"Hiya girls!! Whatcha doin'?"

Whatever our answers were, his response was the same:

"Word?! Wow! That's what's up," accompanied by a hard head nod (this performance continued well into my twenties).

My sisters and I had all the evidence we needed. We decided to write Uncle Muff a letter telling him we knew his dirty, dangerous secret and that we would support him in his transition into sobriety. We wrote it, rewrote it using more supportive wording, and left it in the plastic Ficus outside of his bedroom door.

I imagined him reading the letter, his hand raising an inch with every façade-crumbling word. He emerged from his room with his feet swift and his eyes sullen and charged toward us in slow motion.

"Listen."

We stood at attention, eyes wide.

"I. Don't. Do. Drugs."

I understood that he was lying, and at the time I didn't care to understand why. Maybe he was embarrassed. Maybe he was an adult, so rules didn't apply. Maybe he associated weed smoking with the city where a man with a badge and a gun could use it as a reason to crack your skull. Maybe there on Long Island, where the grass is green and the trees are tall, he felt there was no need for us to accept the restorative rituals of those surveilled by such men or the diligent yuppies along the perimeter of the ghetto.

The After School Specials we were forced to watch would show 'bad' kids in an alleyway wearing snap-back baseball caps. They stood around a younger kid wearing a primary-colored backpack placed firmly on both shoulders and pressed him to stop being lame and take a puff. For me, that boy was my first real boyfriend, Michael. The first time I smoked, I was in his studio apartment in Queens. It was one and a half rooms, save for the bathroom, with a wide screen LED TV

("1080p!"), a solid wood table and chairs, a queen bed on a rolling base, Evisu jeans and long white tees bought in bulk from Chinatown, which in 2006 was a la mode. He was on his own at twenty, and arguably at many points in his life, but his very own place confirmed his professed adulthood and my own, by association. We used to play this Leave it to Beaver game where I would ask to partake in the weed cipher with his friends from my dainty spot in front of the stove or on his bed. He would coolly decline, as expected, saying it was unladylike. Uncle Muff would approve. One particular time, I asked for some, and for whatever reason, Michael said yes. We were alone on his bed and I was wearing a black Italian lingerie set that my Aunt Michelle bought me, about a year or so after Ma discovered birth control pills in my prom clutch. I inhaled a string of fire, sprung up and skip-twitched across the room.

"You got to hold it in. Like this." Michael took a pull and demonstrated what holding one's breath looks like.

Exhale.

"Or you can just swallow it, like this."

And that's how I smoked, all three times a year or so I partook. There was a part of me that liked living sober, a part of me that thought people who wanted to be high or drunk regularly were hiding. I was inexperienced enough to think I would adjust to life more keenly than every other single person who ever lived.

Eventually I started smoking regularly, that is to say, a few shared blunts and a few fucked up white papers rolled for and by myself every week. It started somewhere between breaking up with Michael seven years and two children later, and settling into my first solo apartment in Harlem. My lean expenses equaled my income, and my confidence in being a mother and head of a household equaled zero. I tried charging through these feelings of anxiety by becoming the sort of overzealous mother that I used to watch in black and white on Nick at Nite. I woke up before the sun to make sure their clothes were clean and ironed. I wiped my sons' butts to make sure they didn't miss a spot of shit for far too long into their childhoods. I seldom even said the word 'shit'—"Cheese and crackers," I'd say instead, sometimes in a Midwestern accent to feel more mom-ish.

Inevitably, 'it' will still happen. Be it a past due notice on my apartment door, or cheese-and-fucking-crackers, I sent a peanut butter snack to school. These tiny assaults to my façade reveal to the world that I, the Wonderful Mommy of Oz, am a terrified fraud.

Enter marijuana and its calming effects. To slow down my thoughts and realize I could be doing much worse. I understood why Daddy would call when he was five minutes away from home to tell me to have a 'Twisted Bailey' ready: Grand Marnier and Hennessy with a twist of lemon. This is the same as other adults' sports fanaticism and QVC shopping habits. Unlike excessive shopping or even casual drinking, smoking seemed positive on all fronts.

I'd soon learn just how social smoking weed can be, but in ways I hadn't anticipated. Ma, who I've never seen smoke anything and who I can't picture holding a drink, taught me how to use a rolling machine when YouTube failed me. She remembered how to use it from her younger years, though she doesn't smoke street 'reefer' any longer.

"Where are the seeds?" she asked, shaking her head with her palms facing out as if I was hiding them. "There used to be seeds."

A family friend would wait for an organic batch of weed from her 'guy,' just like she waits for organic apples to go on sale, or to make the trip to Chinatown for her herbal dental mix. All of this pomp and circumstance from a woman who told me she once used heroin. "It was good. It was soooo good." It was so good, in fact, that she understood right then how a person could give up their lives chasing that feeling. Her own father chased that high, which is to say in chasing it he was running from his responsibilities. She enjoyed the high, but knew she would never seek it out again.

I enjoy smoking around my aunt, who tells fluffy, confessional stories when she's loose with secondhand smoke. She declines the mystery green as she tells me that she has tried much worse than GMO marijuana. She describes it as "fun," with not much more detail. She didn't grow up with After School Specials, but with as many casual drug users as devastated addicts. She spoke of it without a hint of longing, but rather with the same satisfaction of remembering a dress she'd outgrown; it was hot at the time, but that time had passed.

I will share none of these gleaming revelations with my children.

"Mommy, there's a cigarette butt in the toilet," my youngest said with his eyebrows furled.

"Really? Well, sometimes the pipes get clogged and stuff comes back up from the sewer."

"The bathroom is smoky."

"The wall vent, baby. Probably the neighbors."

This strategy of lying became more difficult to perpetuate as he became more knowledgeable. And no, it was not about weed:

"Did you know that DC had a superhero named Captain Marvel before Marvel Comics? And, also, do you want to hear something else?"

After a dozen 'something elses,' I respond through clenched teeth with my lips upturned, "Of course."

Before long, I announce that I have to go to the bathroom, and that I shall contemplate if Jean Grey is more powerful than Doomsday as I pee. From the other side of the bathroom door, I would search for a white roach stinking up my bra cup. I spark up—just three pulls is the dosage for philosophical debates on the themes of X-Men, based on a teenage YouTuber's assessment.

The more frequent these conversations, the more frequently someone annoyed me, the more I thought it necessary to see their point of view, the more excusing myself to go to the bathroom became one step too many. I've surely debated that the Avengers would beat the Justice League as I've twisted a grinder and fashioned a filter from the rolling paper container.

More questions from my son, this time not rhetorical:

"Do you smoke cigarettes?"

This time, my answers are more concise: "No. Never. This is different. Real medicine."

On my side was marijuana's recent decriminalization in New York. I sold the idea like it was the equivalent to a portable tumbler printed with 'Mommy's Wine Time.'

"But what about the commercials? What about secondhand smoke? And tar?"

I'd repeat: "This is not like tobacco."

"Actually," Michael smiled, "there's just as much, maybe more tar in a marijuana cigarette." He had the nerve to pretend to be someone who says, "marijuana cigarette".

I gave up justifications for its safety. I stopped waxing poetic about how the plant is the poor man's psychoanalyst. What a treat it is to be high, wind in my ears, green leaves as my halo.

Yet, smoking is hardly the unzipped experience it once was. Years and pounds of smoked herb later, I am no longer Alice in Wonderland. I never feel the need to plant my feet wide on the ground to keep from blowing over. I do not feel one with humanity. I can't close my eyes and be greeted by patterns with meaning. I no longer feel as though my body and my environment are only separated by my desire to maintain some sort of self-containment. I now smoke marijuana for its practical uses. Headache? Smoke. Cranky? Smoke. It is waiting for the work day to cease, for the kids to wind down. Then it's weed-o-clock, time to roll up while crouched over the bathroom sink with one foot keeping the door closed. It's something I hold between my middle and forefinger and flick its ashes with my thumb, it's something I mindlessly blow out of my nose and lament about my burnt sinuses. It's 'I should switch to white papers because blunt wraps are still tobacco, aren't they?' It's the, 'I need to catch some sleep purposeful overdose,' it's the 'I need to write so only five puffs,' it's the 'I have to call the fucking IRS, so let's make the on-hold music my favorite music.' I no longer fall down rabbit holes. I power walk across the plains of my mind, sometimes hitting and descending from bunny hills of enlightenment. I smoke and think of the uncle who fostered my innocence and of my realer-than-most aunt. Of parents who let me know that they were whole people before, during, after, and despite my birth. Coiled in my mind are these people who came before me and every version of myself that has once existed.

More often now, the marijuana high is less of
the literal feeling and more like slowly circling into
myself. The stench now smells like a freshly baked
pie cooling on a windowsill pulling me toward it.
Sometimes it is the only thing that puts me to sleep
once responsibilities begin to plague my mind at
night. I will take what weed has taught me and
translate it to child-friendly practices like self-reflec-
tion. If that doesn't work, I'll tell them to wait until
their twenty-fifth birthday, when their frontal lobes
have completely formed, and we will all take a
wonderful trip. Some people will think this plan is
profound. Others will read it and think it's the
logic of a pothead. Maybe they're right. But maybe
there's profundity in being a pothead.

borderlands

WE PULLED into the driveway in Brentwood, Long Island under a canopy of oak trees. Our new house was a statement compared to our two-bedroom apartment in Brooklyn; there was a cherry tree that wore its onyx bark with restrained dignity, honeysuckle bushes with bright yellow flowers, rabbits scuttling along the perimeter as though they didn't have the good sense to be rats. The ground itself was a novelty, made of equal parts daddy long leg spiders and, as my sister would tell it, crawling things that slid out from under the bushes and into my ears at night. We didn't need the extra space, though we had it. Inside was a stair-case, three whole bedrooms, something called a 'den,' and even a one-bedroom apartment sectioned off on the first floor. And all was quiet. Even the placid shade of brown of the shag carpet and wood paneled walls lent themselves to the ease of nothingness: both absorbed heat from the sunlight spilling through the bay window, making the atmosphere bullishly temperate. Life in the suburbs would be like being wrestled into a long, unexpected nap in the middle of the day.

Hollow suburban air, as clean and fortifying as it was, made some days seem as long as two. With nothing to do and money to burn, some of our neighbors decorated their lawns with a hodgepodge of crap: statues of miniature jockeys holding lanterns, solar powered lights lining driveways, and at least one porcelain dolphin springing upright from a front lawn. Because of this, I likely dismissed the tall wooden frame in the adjoining backyard as decorative, if I had noticed it at all. A few years after we settled in, an atonal scream summoned my sisters and I to climb the treehouse and peer over the fence. The wooden frame was not for a hanging garden or some sort, but for a live goat, tied by its wrists and ankles, stretched like a starfish. The goat pleaded in a language intimated by all species, but its voice got tangled in the oak trees, flattened into oblivion somewhere along the Southern State parkway. Our neighbor was unmoved, neither by the goat's human voice or our hanging jaws, as he prepared the tools for slaughter with the same casualness as he would butter a slice of toast. The scene was misplaced—it belonged among luminescent insects and spiky vegetation and hyper-regional languages. Still, there it all was: shock, steadiness, panic, focus, duty, maybe the faint whistling of an ice cream truck. The screaming stopped. The damned was skinned, broken, drained, fileted. The neighbors must've had meat for weeks. Same if they drove to the supermarket, a straight shot down Islip Avenue.

There were many different types of kids in Brentwood schools. None of whom could pronounce my name, though I learned from theirs that sometimes the letter 'J' is pronounced as an 'H.' Some of these children had parents from places in Central America or the Caribbean, which were governed by thuggish politicians or politically ambitious thugs. Brentwood was an uneventful refuge that didn't force them to get comfortable with English. There were generally two types of teachers in Brentwood public schools: the old white ladies who only exercised their atrophied smiles when the lanky thirty-something superintendent made his rounds, and the excited white recent college grads who kept locked drawers full of candy and reading nooks with bean bag chairs. Both camps saw their role in Brentwood as would missionaries.

When Blacks started immigrating to New York City, the neighborhoods they landed in were flanked and flattened to create an interloping series of roadways that would jettison whites from the five boroughs to more monochromatic townships.

Eventually, Brentwood had become an enclave for Black and brown New York City workers who longed for the quiet and prestige of suburban homeownership. This drop of black, with its corona of brown, pushed the whites into a further surrounding radius, fashioning both a fortress and a noose. The proximity to whiteness is at once an ambition and a healthy fear.

Many of the teachers came from these long lines of New Yorkers, and in their storied, ancestral voices, taught me the regional dialect of Long Island: the word 'all' has a hard 'w,' pronounced 'awl'; the plural of 'you' is 'yous.' Here's how to use these words in action: "I could be teaching in Syosset right now! Instead, I'm here helping awl a yous!" In their voices was an echo of their grandfathers' Brooklyn or Bronx accents, muttering about exactly when the old neighborhood went south.

Some of the kids would hear this, look to their left and right to find mostly brown and Black faces, and gather that their inherent selves and above ground pools were the defining characteristics of a ghetto. By middle school, some of us strove to fulfill this prophecy by accessorizing with yellow and pink bandanas that were left behind by the real gangs, or by naming our cliques something ending with 'mafia' or 'with attitude.' The kids in Ma's residential neighborhood of Rosedale, Queens suffered from the same syndrome, dreaming aloud about when they could accumulate enough money from credit card scamming to "finally get outta the hood," as they scolded their friends for walking on their parents' lawn. As I saw it, if at any moment in your New York life you've been to Home Depot, you are not a child of the ghetto.

Still, there were tidbits of clout that people from Brentwood could scrounge up to assert their roughness. There was EPMD, the eighties rap duo. It didn't matter what they were rapping about, just the fact that they were rapping at all gave us the foundation we needed, the one drop rule. Also, there was the looming threat of violence, which at large was pathetically suburban. We would kill, so to speak, for a rumor of a gun in a locker, or a nineties subway-style razor to the face of some unsuspecting straphanger. In the 'burbs, bomb threats were high fashion. After 9/11, someone realized they could give everyone a day off by calling the school claiming to have hidden an explosive. The ghetto-ass school did not have caller ID, so we would spend the day riding our bikes and enjoying wide, well-paved streets. Even with the news coverage the bomb threats invited, Brentwood schools were still much too good for a Michelle Pfeiffer intervention. Still, I salivated over the plexiglass gyms I saw at other schools while I played bench on the middle school basketball team. One in ten Long Island homes belong to millionaires, which somehow makes one lament about being a part of the nine.

For all the confusion we had about our socioeconomic place in the world, one thing many kids

seemed sure about was their family's cultural
origins. The Puerto Rican kids attempted to make
their distinction clear when they started taunting
the Salvadorians by calling them "Salvys." In
response, the Salvys etched MS-13 tags on lockers
and into benches, giving us the perverse prestige of
assumed gang activity. The Blacks could be divided
into the Blacks who spoke Creole, and the 'regular'
Blacks: just here, being Black, with no home
country or known ties to the American South. For
those of us whose story only went back as far as the
home they grew up in, we had multicultural units
in class which ended with a potluck luncheon.
Other than Black history month, this was the only
time we didn't learn about 'Americans.' Social
Studies was full of 'Americans,' everyone from the
Founding Fathers to Johnny Appleseed. Black
history month, contrarily, was full of 'Black' Americans, and always the same few (I bet you know
who invented peanut butter!) Hyphenated, pref-
aced Americans, not really African or American,
although we live on the soil that our daddy's,
daddy's, daddy lived on, tended to, made flourish.

To decorate the classroom, we were encouraged
to create trinkets that reflected our ethnicities. I
had an indirect feeling that they expected the non-
Caribbean, non-African, non-Southern Black girl
to fashion a drum because bringing turntables as
my ethnic symbol somehow didn't count. It was
Sprite-commercial culture, fine, but was it *culture*
culture? Culture was supposed to be ancient,

grandfathered in and kept afloat by foreign words that infiltrated your speech when you were angry or surprised or secretive. Culture was the clothing you only wrestled into for pictures you took for the family newsletter, for that three day wedding. Culture was a place you flew to every year, not a vacation but just a landing zone you had on some other continent. Even if that place was lush and had clear water and different rules, it wasn't really a holiday, so it's okay if you didn't always enjoy it. Maybe my family could scrounge up enough culture to give it a name, but having to ask almost negated the purpose of the question. I never inquired and made at least one drum fashioned from a tub of Häagen-Dazs.

We were also asked to draw the flag of our family's origin as shown on a giant poster the teacher provided. Not all of the countries were represented, just the cool kids: Western Europe, the major players of East Asia, the parts of South America that keep pre-Columbian languages hidden behind their ears. The American flag may have been on there, but the activity implied we couldn't use it to represent our families, customs or culture. The culture Black Americans have is mixed into the dirt, not to mention that Black is not an ethnicity, only a word—black plague, black magic, black hearted. Blackness felt opaque and borderless, but by no means universal or normative.

I was not South American, not Caribbean as far as I knew at eight years old. My only references to draw upon were staccato anecdotes about Ma's winding family tree: a little Gullah here, a little Nigerian there, the obligatory oral history telenovela about a Cherokee great grandmother. All of this and more mongrelized with lies and poor record keeping. My grandmother spun a tale of a German man floating around our gene pool to which Ma contributed her strong Nordic legs, only to be told by her mother decades later, "German? Where the Hell did you hear that?" Daddy learned even less about his family from his mother, the kind of stiff-lipped parent who didn't tell him about her life in Trinidad, but did give him this gem: always order the cognac. Should the bar you frequent be raided by stick up kids, he could hide his jewelry in the glass of dark liquor.

I scanned the poster for African countries, concluding that it was an obvious place to start. I had no ties to Africa other than my given name, which could be argued as being more African-American in its fumbling association to the mother continent. My eldest sister is named Walida, Arabic for 'first love' or 'newborn child.' Next is Khalila, Arabic for 'intimate friend.' My youngest sister's name is Imani, also Arabic for faith. My name was lifted from Walida's pre-school classmate. It means 'God's friend' in "some West African language," according to Ma and the O.G. Khaholi's mother. I am yet to find it in any Big Book of African Baby Names, and according to Google, it means "Did you mean, Khahli?" Ma even renamed herself at

one point to 'Maatu.' It was around the time she
became a soft-core Hotep and would answer the
phone saying "Peace," the foreignness of it all
making my teeth grind. My first memory of Ma's
reference to Blackness as other than American was
the beaded bracelet she sometimes wore. She
pointed to the beads: "Green for the land, red for
the blood, black for the people." I thought of a
green land made for/by Black people. It was some
place too vague to be more than a daydream.

I continued to scan the poster of flags. There
was the Democratic Republic of Congo: land-
locked and central, the heart pumping the rest of
the continent with backwardness, but otherwise
irrelevant. I knew this because I saw the incessant
Feed the Children commercials: the dusty land, 80
million flies and the one cow everyone in the
country shared. I saw the flag of South Africa. I
knew of that place, too. It had sidewalks and apartment buildings. As far as being African went, I
would settle for either South African or Egyptian,
the latter of which I could not pass for since
everyone knew that Egyptians look like me in the
hieroglyphs, but like Elizabeth Taylor in real life. I
traced a picture of the South African flag above my
name, and avoided looking at it on the bulletin
board over the next few months.

The gray area I found myself lost in was forever
widening, shrinking, and shifting focus. Before our
fifth grade trip to Ellis Island, we had a lesson on
the brave, moldy people who crowded onto boats

and sailed towards the land of opportunity. We saw black-and-white pictures of stoic faces patched with soot and imagined that these immigrants sat on their square trundles to rest their tired feet and to exchange rumors about streets paved with gold. In America they found not gold, but a blinding white. This whiteness was a warm blanket Anglo-Americans kept tangled around their bodies as these kykes, micks and wops went cold in dirt-floor tenements. These off-whites were posthumously integrated, and in 1990, a stone slab etched with some of their names was erected in their honor. The teachers gave us each a strip of paper and a pencil stub to etch the names of our families who made the voluntary passage to the New World.

Once on Ellis Island, I found the slab with the last names that start with 'B' and traced my finger to a group of people with my own last name. 'Bailey,' an English derivative of a French term, meaning a porter or one who resides on the outskirts of the castle walls. That is to say, a professional transient who spent their lives on the outside, to the exponent of slavery. My family may have acquired that name because it was an honorable profession before they elected to come to Ellis Island, but probably not. Using the paper and pencil I made an imprint of these names, thought for a moment, then folded the paper and put it in my pocket anyway. When it was time to leave, the entire fifth grade met up at the agreed upon location. We easily identified each other by our matching T-shirts featuring our town's mascot, the Brentwood Indian: a wise old man in a feathered headdress who, though fictitious, was certainly not from India.

━━

As an adult, I moved to Harlem where the junkies think it's still 1987 and the brownstones are priced for 2050 inflation. Where Hazel Scott played one song on two pianos, where Malcolm preached at Mosque #7, where ideas became literature, where Alpo Martinez and Rich Porter were illuminated and distinguished, where Malcolm died at the Audubon Ballroom, where American dreams are remolded. I moved to Harlem not because of its singular identity, or because my family had a hand in building it, but because of its equidistance from Central and Morningside parks, Restaurant Row and four (*four!*) different subway lines a few blocks away. I was only able to afford the apartment because the government gave my landlord a tax break for corralling the broke people who wish to live on Manhattan Island. Admittedly the housing lottery has a certain funk to it, just as when Harlemites protested the creation of a sewage treatment plant, they were offered the insidious compromise of building Riverside State Park directly on top of it. Instead of my apartment going to a local family who was priced out of their generational home, it was I who fit the comically stringent

income requirements for a two-bedroom walkup
stealthily described as 'being located in' neigh-
boring Morningside Heights.

Approaching my apartment building, I could
hear rats scurrying underneath trash heaps, and
inside my apartment I would hear the mice, their
fear of my approaching footsteps merely performa-
tive. On top of constant squeaking, there was often
screaming all around: of motorcycles revving and
children playing and laughter spilling out of restaurants. In the wee hours, I could hear toothless
couples airing out all of their resentments for each
other and the street life, sometimes unselfcon-
sciously, other times pleading *See me*, only to find
their voices absorbed by cracks in the concrete. But
mostly, my block sounded like oldies blaring from
the street corner at three a.m. on weekdays. I stayed
up many a summer night listening to The Gap
Band and Cameo, waiting for the old New York
trope of an elderly woman in a babushka scarf to
throw a small bucket of trash onto the unofficial
neighborhood DJ.

That never happened, in part because the DJ
was part of the neighborhood's charm. I learned
this from a white couple who were on what looked
like their first date at a sushi restaurant in the neighborhood. I was able to eavesdrop on their conversation because I had long stopped listening to my
own date, an earnest white man who probably
thought he did everything right, handwritten poem
and all, after he nearly broke out in tremors of

indignation as we listened to a Black woman reciting her traumatic American experience at the amphitheater in Marcus Garvey Park.

"I can't move to a neighborhood and call the cops for music playing at two a.m.," the woman said. "It's not my decision to make. I moved into their neighborhood."

Sucker. I haven't called the cops, but I have called 311—the non-emergency line for New York City complaints—at least three times and they are most efficient. But, she was right. It meant nothing to me that the most popular music genre started in part from music played in public spaces, or that the music I sometimes heard meant that the 'perps' were likely in their fifties, or that a stoop or corner is a perfectly reasonable place to form relationships with your neighbors. There's nothing neighborly about the way I behave, nothing connective about how little time I've spent above the iconic and commercial 125th street. Still, to look at me is to see someone who fits in well enough, even if the racial makeup of the zip code is lightening. I reserve the right to cock my head at the white families leaving their single-family residences and think, *thank you for attracting Starbucks, now go home.*

Still, Harlem was their neighborhood, and by racial right, 'my' neighborhood, though some Black people didn't settle there by choice. It became home to many Black Manhattanites who were displaced by racial violence and commercial development in other parts of Manhattan, such as

Chelsea. Some areas were flattened, overtaken, or literally drowned. While every body of water in New York City potentially doubles as a cemetery, remnants of Seneca Village, a Black settlement, softens in the depths of Central Park's Jackie Onassis Reservoir. When empty tenements needed to be filled, a Black real estate agent promised to fill those vacancies. With fewer options than their white counterparts, Black Harlemites were still charged higher rents and more likely to be evicted. Harlem eventually became a sanctioned area for Blacks, meant to contain the people who bore the weight of the oppression, but pain tends to penetrate the air around it. Racism is a shape shifting spot on your back you know just may be the death of you, a rustle in the joints that you couldn't imagine a life without. The residents may have been Black, but the revelers and profiteers were of every color. Harlem was sometimes treated like land where people visited on holiday with seemingly inexhaustible resources but whose economy rests on tourism.

A local church shares this sentiment. They make use of their towering sign on the corner of a popular avenue with evermore brazen messages. In some other context, say, in a zip code where the writers are of a legacy of aggression instead of defensiveness, some of the messages would be considered monstrously divisive. But here, it was ignored or accepted as the ethos of an older institution that long earned its right to be cranky. Once, the sign read something to the effect of, "save Harlem from the gentrifiers and sodomites." I read it just as I read 'MS-13' on a trapper keeper in the early 2000's, translating it as more of a formidable cultural icon than a potential threat. But by 2013, according to the District Attorney, kids in Brentwood were recruited to the very real gang from their English as a Second Language classes, a satellite that orbited the rest of the student body from light years away in a remote wing of the same school. MS-13 seemed to change from phantom to fruition, and Harlem was becoming Chelsea.

I pointed the sign out to my friend, a native Harlemite, and I eked out shocked laughter. Not because the sign was funny, but because laughing was proof that maybe I belonged. I took a picture of the message as self-validation, to record this outrageous New York City sighting, to piecemeal a tribal sense of community. I thought about the people who passed by and read it: the fathers, the artists, the hard of hearing, the homeless, the teachers, the skaters, the red-headed, the bus drivers, the wealthy, the wives, nephews, coaches, screamers, readers, and the loud-music-players. Who did they think Harlem belonged to? I wondered if the people who wrote the message felt confident that they could identify who was who. This land is our land, but never at the same time; whether it's the rent prices or the new neighbors, some of us will leave to build a new home that will be occupied, eventually, by everyone else.

nsync!!!

AS PROMOTED INCESSANTLY, MTV would air an exclusive snippet of NSYNC's No Strings Attached tour as part of their documentary special. My job was to set the VCR and add to one of many VHS tapes we named 'NSYNCage.' We would re-watch their clips, sometimes in slow motion, to find exclusive details within the exclusive content. For the 2000 Video Music Awards for example, one of their backup dancers briefly, but definitely rubbed Justin's dingaling as she danced behind him. Justin looks back, eyebrows furled, before his face relaxes into a smirk and a shrug. So, other fans may have known that Justin drove a cherry red Roadster, or that Joey led a locally successful acapella quartet, but we knew how to approach Justin should we be so lucky.

I tried converting new NSYNC recruits any chance I got, including my 'play brother,' our family friend, Levald. Levald would come by for a visit, answer my questions with questions and to remind us that living in the suburbs was hilarious. "Welcome to Long Island," he would sing, pronouncing "Island" with a hard 'd' like a game show host, every time Jay Z and Cam'ron's 'Welcome to New York City' was on the radio. I knew that NSYNC would be a hard sell to a twenty-something who traded in his Karl Kani persona to become a barefoot vegan back when people were still struggling with the concept of vegetarianism, but being a part of any gang means finding new members. He agreed to watch the exclusive concert clip with me and another resistant convert, Lila.

NSYNC appeared on the screen, welcomed by screaming girls, a sprinkling of boys, and their chaperoning moms. I watched Levald from my seat on the top bunk in my bedroom. It seemed to me that he was torn on whether to find my girlish interest amusing or something of a loss, like some flighty first generation American who can't remember 'real food' from home. The song they sang was the kind of techno-pop that one would expect at a Six Flags concert, but the lyrics, I thought, made up for it. One of the lead singers, JC, co-wrote the song about how fear can control you and how new experiences can be exhilarating and have profound impact on one's outlook in life. It wasn't his fault that it was the title song for a movie tragically named *Space Cowboy*, or that they were wearing the glittering tarp-made pants, or that the choreography made them look like they were riding something, which didn't help dispelling the rumors.

"Like, this is kinda them, but, like, better than this," I reasoned aloud. Why couldn't they sing 'I'll Be Good For You' with its Teddy Pendergrass sample? Or 'I Thought She Knew,' the album's acapella finale to prove, at the very least, that they could sing?

———

I'd like to think that somewhere in the Twilight Zone, there's a dive bar too cool to be named with a tiny stage known for introducing legends. On that stage are five grown men with dyed hair and leather pants so tight they make nothing less than a mangina. They sweat out their synchronized routine to those in the know with a passion and obscurity that earn them the title of Artists.

In reality, they were manufactured in Orlando, where palatable replicas of all things are presented off scale but precise in their detail. NSYNC was constructed as a replica of a replica of a replica.

There was Joey Fatone, the Phat One, a play on his name among other things. The band did not have an official Bad Boy, as none of them did a stint in rehab like some other bands under the same management. Joey did, however, have a baby and a shotgun wedding, a blow to his image that Mani found difficult to calculate: "If he had a baby, then that means..."

Justin, the heartthrob, the youngest and prettiest with the deepest thrusts.

JC was the clear talent of the group, with throaty vocals and a few writing credits. JC was Effie White to Justin's Deena Jones.

There was Lance, the Christian. Lance wasn't branded that way (they were all vaguely Christian, as part of their safe, respectable image), but with his stiff hips and smile, he seemed less passionate about the screaming young women. He sang bass and in my memory, has one solo on the Christmas album. He was there, necessary but not flashy.

Then there was Chris, the oldest (by a lot) and too soprano to sing lead. His voice registers on a frequency that horny teen girls simply cannot hear.

NSYNC and other nineties boy bands, which I shall not name out of loyalty to the former, had captured the hearts and wallets of a demographic still young enough to enjoy the magic of Disney, yet old enough to fix their postures at the smell of a boy's sweat. But why all the screaming? I didn't know how to masturbate, how to distinguish feelings of love from lust. I screamed and danced to the point of crocodile tears to make up for the misplaced moisture.

As much of an affectation as my devotion was, I reserved the right to be offended at the notion that it was a phase, or that I didn't have good taste in music. I needed a sense of progress in the new preteen self I was constructing. Angsty Khaholi was a failure because no one who was supposed to notice, did notice. Likewise, my love for NSYNC was like a monogrammed flask that I took swigs from, waiting for someone to ask what was in it. I was a B-lister in middle school, someone who was the last recruit for the popular table, but sat at it nonetheless. I had no solid clique, so decided to join a global one as a distant comfort. In truth, I would have said I liked anything they put out. NSYNC had an abundance of talent, but fandom wasn't really about what they could do, only how they made us feel.

The song that made me a fan was 'It's Gonna Be Me.' I first heard it as we listened to the radio in art class. Most of us had HOT 97 programmed on the first preset radio button at home, but on heavy rotation was Jay-Z's 'Big Pimpin,' which would have gotten the art teacher fired should the principal hear it through the halls. The video featured a few men and about eight thousand women, some of them taking champagne to the face and loving it. Young Pop n' B acts like Destiny's Child may have been of the same age range as their pop peers, but were marketed as sultry, as was Aaliyah's debut album 'Age Ain't Nothing but a Number,' which Ma played in her rotation along with Toni Braxton's self-titled debut. They all sang moody songs about love that only someone with experience could, and did, create. Forty-something Anita, twenty-something Mariah, and fourteen-year-old

Monica—all grown folk's music. I didn't want to think that marriage might not be a fairytale, or that I would have to one day be my own hero, or to explain to my boyfriend that it's just one of "dem daaayyyys," when I have my monthly mood swings. I wanted to be a child who imagined adulthood, not one actually intertwined with all of its messiness. 'Dirty Pop,' NSYNC's proprietary blend of pop, techno and 808's, was everything I love about pop: simple lyrics, crooning. The Dirty part was the heavy percussion and a reference 'ice' around their necks. The intended effect was for it to go down like milk after cayenne, or maybe a preemptive strike against the inevitable rise of a new Black boy band. By the time B2K rolled around, I had already pledged my loyalty.

I had much catching up to do to be worthy of the term 'fanatic' and set myself apart from the casual fan. Trivia was paramount. Knowing which toothpaste they preferred, or their mother's middle names could earn you memorabilia, which was the second measure of fandom. Mani won all five collectible NSYNC marionettes from the local news station with such knowledge and never let me breathe upon them. We had a Tamagotchi style pocket watch that only displayed snippets of their videos. There were posters, magazines, candy, and more NSYNC specials to record and re-watch in slow motion, slower, slower, until we discovered NSYNC fact #873: they probably don't wear underwear beneath their sweatpants.

Their final album, 'Celebrity,' had a roster of respected producers, namely The Neptunes, whose claim to fame was making beats for forever-hits like N.O.R.E.'s 'Super Thug.' The Neptunes produced their single 'Girlfriend,' a smooth and easily work-able beat that was in line with the group's hazy yet identifiable credibility strata once their hit 'Gone,' was on regular rotation on POWER 105.1, "New York's Hottest Hip Hop and RnB." 'Girlfriend' was one of my favorite tracks on the album. It was a warm, intoxicating balance of masculine commands and desperate pleas. The video for 'Girl-friend' opens to a crowd of young adults in a junk-yard and the boys in skull caps and hoodies. There's Justin, making eyes at a Black love interest! JC's is Asian! Joey sat with a brown woman, possibly Hispanic with straight, or straightened, hair. It was a wilted salad of cultural pandering served right before we would get back to the white meat. As palate cleansers, Chris and Lance each have blondes.

I didn't want to notice this. I didn't want to admit how much I hated the fact that I loved the song, because it seemed aimed somewhere near my vicinity. I wanted to pretend I didn't know what it all meant, just like the time I read aloud from a Rolling Stone article that their melodies were African American derived and asked Ma to trans-late, though she only rolled her eyes. I saw the strategy when watching their twice removed prede-cessors New Kids on the Block; they did not create the song to gain more Black fans, but fans who think Black music is cooler without Black guys. It was part of NSYNC's final image and sound, one I thought was made to solidify them as mature. After that, the only place to go was away.

JC went solo and led with the single featuring Little Baby Jesus, or Ol Dirty Bastard, as most may remember as his original name in the Wu Tang Clan. If any member could have been on that imaginary dive bar stage with a growl that would challenge the sound system, it was JC. What he did not have was the lust in his eyes that we fanatics worshiped in Justin. He was in a no man's land of teeny bopper alums who found it impossible to reinvent themselves without a crisis of religion or sexuality.

Lance trained and campaigned to be one of the first civilians launched into space. He wasn't chosen, I feel in part because his possible death would have been bad PR for NASA. Also, he came out as gay. I had an hunch when a magazine interviewer asked them all what they found attractive in a woman. One member said eye contact. Another mentioned confidence. Lance said, "her stomach."

Chris was already at retirement age and seemed to do just that.

Justin went from Dirty Pop to Contemporary Urban. He went so far as to nearly name his debut album 'Blue Eyed Soul,' which would have been fitting. His debut solo album, 'Justified,' could be enjoyed with many generations of R&B lovers, as I often did. It featured prestigious and of-the-moment collaborations, melodic parallels to Stevie Wonder, lyrics intended for Michael Jackson and a nineties style ballad. An eight out of ten classic. Still, his critics implied he should pick a side: he was Black when he performed with Janet, white when he threw her under the bus. Black again with 'Suit and Tie,' white again with 'Man of the Woods.' This does not mean the artist doesn't earnestly love and respect Black music. It means that American music is largely Black music.

Joey went to Broadway. As a self-professed loud Italian from Brooklyn, he had the personality and a steady mezzo soprano to rightfully be cast as the lead singer. By the time he joined NSYNC, however, Joey Fatone was (not so) cleverly deemed the 'Phat/Fat One,' and was relegated to "Ooooohs" and "Ahhhhs" on the background track. After NSYNC, Joey sought to regain his position as a lead by starring in plays, which made him much more accessible. I decided to take the train to Times Square when he and the cast of the play were slated to give a promotional performance.

I got dressed in my Celebrity World Tour tee, ripped and resewn, and adorned my braids with red rubber bands. I purchased the shirt at their concert a few years prior, a disappointing experience I was hoping to reframe. Daddy bought tickets for Mani and me to attend the show at Giants Stadium, which we mentally prepared for with the seriousness of a pilgrimage. We found our seats and took a look at our extended family in pop. We sat behind a pasty family decked out in impressive memorabilia, but without smiles; they looked like coming-of-age Amish on leave from the community to sow their oats. Behind us sat another family with tight jaws and soulless eyes that seemed to meet mine whenever I turned around. Mani and I looked at each other, smiling hard and raising our shoulders, trying to keep the spark kindling though disenchanted by our lack of community. The lights went low and five cloaked men appeared on the stage. The pyrotechnics hit, and then the dancing. Mani and I stood up as I tried my best to squeeze a tear from my eyes. We grew up watching Michael Jackson concerts on VHS and marveled how full units of EMTs were present to pull fainted fans out of the stands, and I was there to get things started for my boys. An all-stadium tour for an album that was yet to be released was not enough; someone needed to be hauled out on a stretcher.

"Could you please sit down?" asked the dead-eyed adult behind us, and so we did, the entire time. We enjoyed the concert with our hands in our laps, nodding along to songs that we didn't know.

As I approached the budding festivities, a grown woman in business attire was shouting without shame from fifteen feet away, "JOEY! JOOEEEYY!! How's your daughter, Briana?! Jooooooey! Joooooey!" Her tone wavered between pleading and taunting, but Joey ignored her so thoroughly it was as though he couldn't hear her at all. Typically he seemed restricted, a natural front man who may have exploded into confetti if kept in the back too long. But as the star of his current endeavor he was muted, casual, in his element to the point that he almost seemed like a human being. He stood close to the barricade and began speaking casually with a young adult couple. They looked like they knew each other, or as I saw it, they came to him so smoothly, so normally that he felt like a person, not a commodity to dump their fantasies on. I would do the same. I wasn't bat shit crazy, I was an admirer of his work. Once the conversation broke, I took my opportunity in one long breath:

"JoeyI'myourbiggestfancanItouchyour-hand???"

I stretched my hand out to him and waited. And waited. He stared at it. Joey seemed stunned, somehow, and the couple looked down as rays of embarrassment shot from my pores. Joey said nothing and turned his back to me.

Maybe it was that he was no longer a celebrity, but an artist. Artists don't need the sweaty palms of girls who see them as a face of a Pog they must collect, for no other reason than there are five in the set. All he seemed to want was a collapsible stage on a midtown side street in the daytime, a little bit of the spotlight and a song to sing.

Maybe Joey was just another tired employee who pointed to the clock when a late customer arrived. I had to realize that the theme park is made for the thrill, but under the costumes are child-support-paying, fibroid-having adults who rub their feet as they ride the shuttle bus to the parking lot. Joey's shift as boy band member #4 was over, and after hours meet and greets were above his pay grade, ma'am. Come back during our normal hours.

NSYNC's heyday was from 1997 until about 2002, long enough for me to get to the other side of puberty. My love for them was so far from reci-procity that such a relationship could be deemed parasocial. Still, fandom provides a twist of sophis-tication in that it surpasses our immediate thirst for love and attention (which we delay by focusing on a stranger), and strips it bare to the only lasting ecstasy: desire. If desire represents the possibilities of the future, then requited love represents the known, and eventually, disappointment. Once the object of that desire is up close, you notice the blemishes on their skin, a glint of insecurity in their smile. A total Monet.

I let go of Joey from my gaze and my CD rota-tion. It was time to grow up and seek tangible expe-riences and deeper relationships, to understand that having something is more satisfying than desiring it, even though what I have will deteriorate or otherwise change in ways that are less predictable than the chords of pop. I walked to the subway, quietly consoling myself with the fact that the Fat One had no solos. I was at once humiliated and free.

new words

AS A CHILD, there was a time when I couldn't open my mouth without cursing. It started when I was about seven or eight, and caught a scene of the classic *House Party* on cable. The love interest stood in front of Kid (the high-yellow one) of the duo Kid N' Play and told him if he ever lied to her, she would "kick his ass." Of course, I had heard the phrase before, but she made it sexy. He nodded, near hypnotized as she threatened him again and again. 'Ass' only opened me up for clunky deuces I would drop, more 'shits' than on a car parked under a tree.

In safe places like the school hallway or cafeteria, other kids would share meditations on such words. Did you know Shakespeare invented the word 'fuck'? Yep. Forced Unlawful Carnal Knowledge. No? Then it's Fornication Under Consent of the King. You've seen *Braveheart*, right? Shakespeare did use the word 'firk,' which meant to strike, but was used as slang for sex. We have since expanded the heartless analogy with 'smash,' 'bang,' 'screw' and 'beat up.' If one didn't like that definition, one could still use 'fuck' as an exclamation after stubbing one's toe, to connote if a person or thing is desirable or, if you say it with some stank on it, very undesirable. There are no less than eight thousand other applications.

In the early 2000's, Michael and I fucked in his messy bedroom. It might have felt good if I wasn't staring at the venetian blinds, stunned by the fact that we were doing 'it.' 'It' was fucking, because 'making love' was for people in their forties, or the pivotal scene in a romantic movie. We weren't in a movie; we were on a squeaky mattress in Queens. Michael did, however, send me home in a cab and not on the bus, so maybe we did make love? His upbringing being much less quaint than mine, skipped over the part of childhood when fantasy and expectation are the same. He rejected the notion many times with a half smile: "No such thing."

The firking kept up, and years later mine and Michael's son, Aiden, sat in his booster seat and proved he was bilingual. Basic English, compassion and humanity has no place in Manhattan traffic.

"Fuckin' douche bag," he said before I could.

"Fuckin' is the same as fuck." I reminded him of the time I told him, to his surprise, that 'fuck' was a bad word. He had said it so fluidly. Elegantly, even.

"It is?"

"Yes. And douchebag isn't the nicest word, either (refer to On Morality and Marijuana, and my implementation of the phrase 'cheese and crackers')."

Aidan also knew how to classify his older brother, MJ, before I wanted to abbreviate him with a label. At a playgroup, MJ knocked down another kid's block tower, which took forever (twenty minutes) to create. The playgroup was for other autistic kids and their families looking for a respite from the insensitivities of the playground, the children's museum, the beach, street fairs, and every other place that is made for screaming and rough housing, but to an extent. MJ would grab other children's food out of their hands, run away without direction or heed to safety, and dive into big women with low cut tops as if they were ball pits. At least at special-needs playgroup, I wouldn't have to apologize excessively. Before I could assess whether the kid's anger was justified, Aiden wedged himself and his teddy bear between the boy and MJ and said, "Leave him alone! He's autistic!"

MJ does not call me "Mom." He doesn't call me anything. 'Autism' was the word the doctor gave us, an upgrade from the previous diagnosis of Pervasive Developmental Disorder, Not Otherwise Specified, or PDD-NOS. A clear diagnosis should have given us a sliver of guidance more than the

unknown, but learning that autism exists on a spec-
trum did little as far as my understanding. Some
people with autism lead typical lives, perhaps with
an atypically organized room. Others with autism
could care less about hyper categorization, and have
no problem being touched, as per the preconceived
notion. Some people with autism will find cate-
gories for every little thing, placing their toys in
order and integrating their intersectionality like
shape, color, or usage. Some autistic people speak
concisely and passionately. Others, like MJ, hardly
speak at all.

Speaking ability is of course different from
receptive language skills. Imagine understanding
English, but the moment you try to respond, no
matter how hard you try, you respond in Greek. MJ
would bang his head in frustration, or another
autistic kid put, "try and get words out." MJ can't
yet tell me why he bites his forearms, or if he's
bothered as much as I am by his erratic sleep
patterns. I let other autistic people speak for him, as
well as devices with electronic cards with pictures
on them that Siri can read aloud. If Alex cannot say
mother with his own voice, can I ensure that he
knows the implications behind that word? If I'm
not "mother," is there no understanding of the
misery and triumph of labor, of rote but taxing,
often background work? No "father," no sense of
security? If I envision a grand piano, does MJ
imagine a synthesizer?

Without a singular definition, and as it often

goes when one is immersed in attempting to understand a condition, I've wondered if I'm autistic as
well. As a kid, I hardly ever spoke up. All that
cursing was done at home and around friends.
Otherwise, silence was my default mode. My repu-
tation was such that other grade schoolers, whom I
never formally met, would walk up to me and ask,
"why are you so quiet?" and I would just stand
there, quietly.

I suppose they wanted to know why I
wouldn't speak up even when it was necessary.
Like when a hair stylist once asked me why I
didn't say anything when she discovered water
running down my back after she shampooed my
hair. Or at the end of that hectic day in fourth
grade when I couldn't get the teacher's attention
for the bathroom pass. I opted to stay in the classroom, wholly unnoticed, until my bladder
exploded onto my new cream-colored leather skirt.
I walked calmly to the girls' room with a full
stream of pee splashing my ankles. I dried off,
went back to class, and claimed whoever smelt it,
dealt it.

The answer to that question that I had adopted
in time was, "I just don't have anything to say to
you," which did nothing but preserve a crumb of
pride. That's probably why I decided to integrate
my home and school personae with a small group
of girls, huddled in a circle on the grass in someone's backyard. We each went around and said one
curse word each, looked down at the grass and

giggled. I think I said "damn," the pussiest of the lot.

I resorted to selective mutism because I much preferred my native tongue: a Creole of half words and household slang with no gaps for breath, spoken only by me and my sisters. When we wanted to play with our Barbies but were old enough to be embarrassed by it, we played 'Marvs' instead, which was playing Barbie, except renamed for one of the perps in Home Alone. When we learned how to play the card game Spades, its jargon became the root of a new dialect in our household.

In the game, spades are the dominant suit but only after all cards of other suits have been played, delivering a metaphor so complete that I wonder if that was why it became popular with Black Americans. In its official context, spade is derived from the Italian *spada*, a type of sword. If the initiating player throws down a heart, for example, and another player does not have any hearts, she can 'cut' with a winning spade. One can also cut with the Two of Diamonds, which we will consider an Adam Clayton Powell among the ranks.

'Cut' became 'slice' and slice became the default for all fails and insults. That was, until the temporary siblings (the perk of being the product of young, attractive divorcees), picked up the word. Any other kid pointing and shouting slice at one of my sisters was enough reason for our flimsy bond to bend. Slice was ours. For Us, By Us, as was the word 'renegger.' If one of us reneged (illegally played a spade) she was a renegger. Naturally, we replaced the -er with an -ahhhhhh, and shot it out of our mouths like pellets. The words change how we are perceived, just as how we are perceived can inform the words we use.

My intersectionality—Black, female, mom, daughter, heterosexual, etc.—expresses to an extent who I am. Having a widely recognized term to describe myself is better than being undefined and therefore unseen, unimportant. Still, labels trap us in its parameters and implications, even unintentionally. For example, a color is not a land or a lineage and therefore not a race, and so identifying as Black may imply that we are well behind the finish line. The word black has changed over time, once meaning 'pale' until the sixteenth century. Similarly, if it were the 1500's, I would have referred to both of my sons as girls, as all young children were. 2023, the year of writing this, seems to be the horizon of a time when children are tasked with coming to their own conclusions about gender. Without an empirical determination, it would imply that they must base their opinions, at least in part, on the platitudes that propelled us to make changes in the first place.

Our bodies and ourselves become even more separate by the passive language we adopt. I am yet to adjust to hearing the word "bodies" in lieu of "people." 'Black bodies come in a vacuum-sealed pack, something you leave next to your car keys so that you won't misplace them. Though the term seems to be exclusively used when someone is defending the worth of Black bodies, the coldness of the term has an opposite effect of the space in which the conversation is sanctioned.

Further, we move within 'spaces' now, not places. A place is finite and has a definite set of rules: no cursing in the classroom, no clean language in the yard during recess. Meanwhile, a space is for you and your purple circle of emotions, space so we can't touch, space so that it can be redefined faster than you can observe. So much unbound area that all there is to do, eventually, is to bump into each other, to meld into each other. Everything, eventually, becomes the opposite of itself—the word for pale became the word for dark; girls became boys, who could become women; laugh so hard you cry; experience a devastation so profound all there is to do is find its humor.

Words do not matter to the extent that they change over time. To MJ, I may never be "mommy," but I'm still the person he goes to for a hug, who he hid behind when the geese in the park got too close. I call my mother "Ma," which she repeats when she hears it, her younger self in disbelief that she can be identified by a one-syllable caw. To me, it's not a reduction, more of an omnipotence. "Ma" and its derivatives are the same as a look of hunger, a tug on the hem of a dress. Just as whether it's called "fucking" or "firking," the act remains the same.

in transit

WE WOULD WAIT for the train on an elevated platform beside the blue of the sky. Ma would step onto the raised yellow strip that marked the edge of the platform and peer down the track looking for the next train toward Manhattan.

"Ma!"

She would edge back whenever she was satisfied with whatever she saw, never justifying my fear. That didn't stop me from imagining that Ma could be here, then soundlessly fall off the platform and into oblivion. Once the train arrived, she was never aggressive, but her moves were exacting, demanding in her surety, in her grip of the spaces between.

I never knew where we were going when we rode the subway, and it didn't matter. Ma knew the subway. Where to transfer, how to spot a drunk from the far side of the train car and to move to the next one. It was odd how much Ma belonged there, riding alone since she was seven or eight. I watched her surrounded by blackened gum and advertisements placed overhead to reduce eye contact and fights between passengers. "Don't touch the railing." "Don't touch the bench." "Do not feel guilty when a grown man asks you for money." It wasn't prudish: it was survival. The abrasiveness of the environment didn't make her jagged or jaded but buffed her to a high shine. Soft skin, softer demeanor. Her stature and everything she did became the definition of femininity. All 115 pounds of her would face the riptide of people exiting the train, sometimes three of her youngest children behind her. No one dared to bump us or cheat us out of a seat. And if they did, Ma later assured us, in an anecdote about an ex, that she could fight: "If you're a woman fighting a man, everything is fair. Bite him." The elevated train would gain speed as it cut through the boulevard, the taller buildings eclipsing into the next until they all melded together into a pattern of red bricks and patches of light. Stop, go, stop, go.

The subway functions for and despite the people, a symbiotic relationship founded on mutual curtness. The subway runs twenty four hours a day, seven days a week. It can bring you from the tip top of the Bronx at Riverdale to the southern shores of Far Rockaway for a low price, or free if you're agile enough, but part of the price is paid with each dodge of sludge that began culturing on a leaky ceiling sometime in the early eighties. The New York City subway is not for the nice. It's where no one cares about you or where you're trying to go, where you may wait on the same platform and see the same people every day and never get to know them, where altruism is whittled into the shanks that are weaponized elbows. On a busy staircase, I learned to walk so closely to you that I will scuff your shoe and tip it off your foot. The able-bodied will steal glances at a person to decipher if they are elderly enough to deserve their seat; sixty four year-olds can stand and laboriously readjust their bags as seated youths pretend to power nap through the smell of their sweat and drudgery.

We ignore many things on the subway, like the corner of the platform that looks like a giant pimple burst, but other things we must stop and take notice of because it sharpens our environmental skills. Knowing immediately that the pile of shit you passed is dog or human could inform your next moves. The workers of the Metropolitan Transit Authority certainly try; the trash cans are always emptied in a timely manner, mops are dragged across the train car floors. But cleaning is futile in a city that contains a man I once saw lay across a store front and pee across a quadruple-wide Times Square sidewalk during rush hour. The filth extends to the many living examples of how life can be unpredictably cruel. Then, the cruelties become predictable, compounded.

From Brooklyn, the three youngest siblings almost went with Ma to Georgia. But first she gathered money and the nerve to order a moving truck to arrive when Daddy was at work. Ma would make the exodus from the cold, expensive city just as her sisters and brother did. Ma called her siblings and set up a place for herself and her daughters in Atlanta. We would grow up with our cousins eating smothered biscuits and puberty would bring fat to our thighs in a way bagels could not. We would grow up without snow days or Sundays on the Brooklyn Heights promenade, or oils on folding tables on Atlantic Avenue, or the ability to hop on a train underneath traffic and avoid eye contact with strangers. We would be sheltered by grass and swamp and the relative normalcy of growing up with a single mother.

The moving truck came. The driver called the house. Daddy was not at work, and Daddy picked up the phone. Ma was stuck, but Daddy always knew where he was going, at least as much as men who don't like to ask for directions.

Daddy never took the subway. He is far from pretentious, just too autonomous to deal with panhandlers and a schedule he didn't create. Daddy rode his bike instead. I remember hearing a story of how he rode across the Brooklyn Bridge with Lila attached to an infant seat on the back of his bike. They had ice coming from their nostrils and smiles on their numb faces. The freezing East River underneath attached to them, though not strong enough to pierce the comfort and triumph of getting to the other side.

Daddy called a real estate agent and moved his three daughters to Long Island. Three girls, one parent, one Doberman. The white minivan. Honeysuckle bushes. Pines with wretched arms. Mommy on the Long Island Railroad at Atlantic Terminal, to the transfer hub in Jamaica, Queens, and finally to Brentwood, Long Island, and back again. In the divorce agreement, she let her being seep into the cracks, giving her every other weekend with us and some bills to pay.

———

Instead of a house in Atlanta, Ma moved into her first apartment as a newly single woman, as a Mom, but not quite a Single Mom. On our visits we always took the train with Ma, hailed cabs, walked on sidewalks and discovered restaurants along the way. City things. Cooler than normal, but abnormal nonetheless.

One of her first post-divorce apartments was in a brownstone. Each floor was occupied by one tenant, but the floor plan was like a floor of a single-family home. We could leave the kitchen, walk down the semi-communal hall to get to the next of her private rooms, which were all attached. It was always a little too dark and felt exposed when we heard the other tenants walking up the staircase, a fleeting but definite stake in our realm. Ma left that place quickly because she predictably had been harassed by another tenant.

Her last apartment was in Downtown Brooklyn, in a six-story building wrapped in vine across the street from the Brooklyn Academy of Music. Everything was around her apartment and in it: the smell of Turkish coffee from the restaurant downstairs, the pulse of the drums during the Dance Africa Festival, which was further cultivated by Ma's committed yet short-lived House music phase. Sometime after she got settled in her place, her partner, Alec, moved in. Though with the entire city growing into her windows, romanticized by the smell of Alec's freshly made waffles on Sunday mornings, it feels more appropriate to say she took a lover. Alec and Ma looked like they were created from the same ethereal batch, both short, soft spoken and long thinking. He helped redecorate with framed copies of minstrel show ads and other throwbacks to America's formative years, in which I tried to find the solace of irony or Ma's own taste.

She soon bought a Tudor row home in Queens. Alec made it to leasing but not much further, their life projections going in two different directions. Ma didn't need to travel the same road of marriage and children again. Too many turns, too many thorns on the path.

In tenth grade, I moved in. Queens was in New

York City, and New York City was exciting. No one was like me in Brentwood, anyway, and I chalked that up to my life of sophistication, namely my need to eat crusty, chewy, authentic bagels and not the previously frozen discs the cafeteria served. I was the outlier, not humble enough to be the wild-card any longer. New York City was for people who wanted to be someone, although with the sheer number of people, everyone was no one. But Rosedale, Queens was the last town in the city limits, a suburb of Jamaica, which felt like a suburb of Manhattan. Rosedale had no subway station, no designated walled place to take public transportation with dignity and indulge in the anonymity of a big city. Instead, I waited daily at a degradingly situated bus stop on the corner of a major intersection. I stood and waited for the Q85 bus while passersby did not adhere to the rules of the subway; instead, people stared, waved, and honked.

When we were all grown up and bouncing around the city on our own, we told Ma that there's nothing wrong with moving to Atlanta with her sister, Karen. She still had a dream where we were all running to catch the bus, but she missed it as the only one carrying all of our baggage. We told her to drop our bags and run. So, she picked out a house. The plan was for her and Karen to visit the farmer's market on weekends, to reminisce about their childhoods and discuss waning motherhood. Ma would continue all of her hobbies—knitting, design, inventions and voice over artistry, each taking up the spaces between work, children, and illness. Projects were deemed unfinished until the guilt of abandonment would creep up and bother her, and she would then consider it discarded. The project never really mattered in the first place, only having the courage to start. But in this new place of exhalation, this last era of adulthood, she may just complete it.

Aunt Karen came to New York as they were solidifying plans. We went to a jazz show in the Village and then walked miles afterward, stopping at shop windows and making easy conversation. Lila and I told her she was never as beautiful, as big breasted and round hipped as she was that night. We stopped a man to pet his thoroughbred, a dog with fur flecked with silver like the underside of leaves before a storm. Aunt Karen mentioned that she read of this terrible rare sickness, in which a dog can infect a human with a flesh-eating disease. How unlucky would that be?

Ma's moving plans halted for a moment to pay respects to her late Aunt Esther. The funeral was to be held at a cathedral in Brooklyn.

"Be careful," Aunt Michelle said. "Somebody will start fighting."

"Why?" my sisters and I asked.

She and my mother put their hands up as if to say it takes too much energy to explain the dynamics of grief, sibling rivalry and, apparently, tradition.

"Just sayin'."

Aunt Esther's children and grandchildren arrived at the service vested in white. Their sadness was palpable; they seemed like bundles of skin stripped raw, helpless to the tiny needle pricks of each passing particle of air. Friends took to the podium and laughed about how Aunt Esther would use her work badge to join parades and gain VIP access to events. The pastor spoke of her daughter's devotion—spiritual, physical and emotional. The speaking stopped, the organ played, and said devoted daughter flew off the front pew and ran screaming with balled fists toward her older sister.

After the repast, Lila, Aunt Michelle, Ma and I walked the familiar Brooklyn blocks toward Ma's old apartment in front of the Brooklyn Academy of Music. Aunt Michelle lived there at the time, and Lila would soon inherit it. It was 'The House' in Brooklyn, where we met up and fried whiting while listening to Chaka and Aretha and Dr. Buzzard's Original Savannah Band. Our bubble was the same, though Brooklyn was slowly turning into Manhattan: tall, mirrored buildings here and there, white people venturing past gerrymandered partitions for the first time in generations. Still remaining were the three-story brownstones, a few cobblestone streets. There were newer murals commissioned with corporate money, others created by loved ones of those departed along with prayer candles and pictures, though the latter was collected on trash day. We finally discussed Aunt Karen. Before they would buy a house in Atlanta, she just needed a quick detour to the cancer treatment center in Florida. I had known she was sick for months by then, that she was diagnosed right after we saw her at the jazz show. It was the first time I let myself think that she was really sick.

We rounded Ashland Place. We turned the corner, the same corner we had turned for years, except this time we hit a glossy, cold monolith, for commercial and residential use. We stopped in this monster's shadow, eyebrows heavy, mouths crooked and for the first time let our confusion melt into grief:

"What's happening to Brooklyn?"

━━

I took the Mega Bus down to Washington, DC. The Florida plan didn't work out, so Aunt Karen stayed at a hospital closer to her home. The hospital had signs posted in every elevator that boasted of its accolades which gave me confidence, as did Aunt Karen's comfortably sized room. Everyone was already there, seeming to have a good time as we always did. I sat on the window seat and smacked on chicken that Aunt Karen's best friend, Ann, basted with sweet onions. We argued over which one of us would marry Anthony Mackie. My cousin twisted Aunt Karen's hair and talked about the hair grease she applied and the technique she adopted: "It'll last for weeks." We marveled and pretended not to notice Aunt Karen's yellow eyes. When the doctor came in, I didn't try to understand; it would have been like starting a movie when it was halfway over. But others listened intently, skeptically maybe, but only because this was too important to trust just anyone. When Aunt Karen spoke everyone hushed to listen, but we didn't crane our necks, or put our hands to our ears. After all, we were simply eating and talking and cracking jokes. Aunt Karen had to use the restroom, so her daughter helped her up, and the only curve I could make out from under her hospital gown was her spine.

A month or so later Aunt Karen was discharged back to her apartment where I joined her and the rest of our family. Her weight was back up but only in water pooled by her ankles. Her voice was no louder than the sound of her home settling. Her eyes were loud yet calloused, her expression like watching yet another apocalypse on a television screen. More onion-basted chicken. The twists in Aunt Karen's hair were still tight and swingy. Every hour I peered into Aunt Karen's bedroom to see everyone still as they were the last time I checked. Then idleness. Awkward spaces. Stepping over people to offer help. Of course I can move the ottoman. Refill the ice tray? You got it. I convinced myself that playing Mario Bros with my nephew was helping. We played the original game on its original console, not one made for Nintendo 64 or better, with its nauseating 360-degree view. The classic version had two dimensions, allowing a player to only go forward and backward, until the world behind your character is zipped up and gone.

Ma asked Lila and I to iron the linen, a benevolent chore. We ironed and folded it, then I saw my cousin, Aunt Karen's son, standing in the hallway with his arms folded and his eyes somewhere unseen.

"Do you need anything?" I asked. He stared, then shrugged. "I know, I know," I said, then went back to the room and unfolded the linen. It will be wrinkled, there's a bunch in the fold. We decided to roll it instead of folding it.

"Should I fold it in half?" I looked at my sister. "I'm buggin', right?"

Lila laughed. "We could fold it again in half. Should we put up the ironing board?"

"But where will we place the linen?"

That winter, instead of Atlanta, we all went back to Brooklyn where Aunt Karen grew up. We talked about how big my sons were over coffee and hot chocolate. We walked along the river facing the Manhattan skyline which never stopped sparkling, even though Aunt Karen's ashes were in a paper carton in Ma's hands. Some of us said a few words we thought of beforehand, others shouted love as we dropped her ashes into the East River. Some parts of her may have grouted in the sediment, some parts flowing out into the Atlantic Ocean, parts of Aunt Karen infused in our tap water, in the food that we eat.

Ma still planned on moving. But before she sold the house in Queens, she was just going to paint the bedrooms, quickly have the living room ceiling patched, strip the insulation from the kitchen and replace the walls. Brick and wooden planks were exposed, and person-sized rolls of insulation stood in the corners of the kitchen, but soon everything was mended, mostly by her own hands. She brought linens to stage the place for potential buyers to better envision their lives there, a fantasy without dust, overflowing hampers, or disagreeable neighbors. This house would be their destination, and they would never have a reason to leave.

As she prepared to go, I prepared to be without her. I reminded myself that Ma was the embodiment of home, so it didn't matter where she would settle. She would still burn incense and anchor it with the soap bottle on the edge of the kitchen sink. Sometimes it would burn down and stain the edge of the sink with an indented streak of a fire that once was and will be again. I stain my windowsills in the same fashion, a sort of talisman. In my own travels, her voice would forever act as my conscience, especially as I ride the subway and listen to its charming patrons.

"Can anybody help me not be broke?" a homeless man asked the entire subway car. "I don't mean no harm, but I'm trying my best to not be broke any more."

I consoled myself for being tightfisted. I worked for that dollar.

"I am a human," he continued, now halfway down the subway car. "If I was white it'd be all good. But y'all think I belong in a cage."

I look up to see who else has looked up. I caught the eye of a woman who looked back down, unbothered. I did the same. It's a tactic from our chimp encoding, emphasized by the bloodletting that is New York's concentrated self-preservation.

No one knows this better than subway performers. I once enjoyed a drum-playing singer behind shy eyes, trying to mask the whimsy growing in my chest for his voice and lyrics. I thought about giving him a dollar, then lamented for every time I didn't give one to a person who was starving for food and human contact. I turned down the music in my earbuds but kept them lodged in my ears to stay in character.

In his song he made a joke that no one under-stood except the man standing in front of me, who was leaning on the subway doors (a bonus way of being ignored is to try and get on or off the train while another passenger idly blocks the doors). The man had his earbuds in as well, but seemed to hear the song and the joke quite clearly.

"Did anyone get it? You got it," the drummer said directly to the man, but the man stared at his phone, ignoring him. The drummer grew tired of giving without satisfaction:

"You look at me but if I look back at you, you look away. It's not the politicians that are the problem, it's us. We're afraid to connect."

The man still didn't look up. I was hoping the performer could make out the reflection of my eye contact in the plastic ad panel in front of me. When he didn't, I turned to him and said "thank you," after he bid us all a good day.

He said nothing. Fuck him. I left the train and stepped over the gap and onto the platform. I leaned over and looked for the next train. Don't fall.

acknowledgments

To my family—I am forever grateful for the power each of you have granted me through your encouragement and support. I am made better by your infinite curiosity, wisdom and love. Because of each of you, I understand what true wealth is.

To Leza and Christoph of Clash Books—thank you both for your faith in me, for your love of art without pretense or permission. I am truly honored to have met you.